YES, YOU CAN SING!

LEARN TO SING WITH LESSONS FROM ONE OF THE WORLD'S TOP VOCAL COACHES

YVIE BURNETT

WITH RICHARD BARBER

JOHN BLAKE

YVIE BURNETT studied at the Royal Scottish Academy of Music and Drama in Glasgow, Guildhall School of Music & Drama in London and the National Opera Studio, specialising as a mezzo-soprano opera singer, before going on to perform as a soloist in operas around the UK and Europe. She first came to the attention of TV audiences in 2005 as a vocal coach on *The X Factor*, a show she worked on for six series. She has also worked on TV shows including *Britain's Got Talent*, *The Voice UK*, *America's Got Talent* and *Let it Shine*, and has provided coaching and guidance to some of the world's biggest stars such as Sam Smith, Leona Lewis, Katy Perry, Susan Boyle and Sarah Brightman.

RICHARD BARBER has edited a number of magazines including *Woman's Realm* and *OK!*, for both of which he won the British Society of Magazine Editors' Editor of the Year, as well as *Woman* and *TVTimes*. He wrote the unofficial biography of Earl Spencer; the Sunday Times Top 10 bestseller, *Unbeaten*, detailing the life of *How Clean Is Your House?* presenter Kim Woodburn, and *Annie's Song*, the life of the Nolans' eldest sibling, Anne. He lives in North London with his wife, Patti.

Published by John Blake Publishing Ltd,
3 Bramber Court, 2 Bramber Road,
London W14 9PB, England

www.johnblakebooks.com

www.facebook.com/johnblakebooks ⬛
twitter.com/jblakebooks ⬛

This edition published in 2017

ISBN: 978 1 78606 413 4

British Library Cataloguing-in-Publication Data:

A catalogue record for this book is available from the British Library.

Design by www.envydesign.co.uk

Printed in Great Britain by CPI Group (UK) Ltd

1 3 5 7 9 10 8 6 4 2

Papers used by John Blake Publishing are natural, recyclable products made from
wood grown in sustainable forests. The manufacturing processes conform to the
environmental regulations of the country of origin.

Every attempt has been made to contact the relevant copyright-holders, but some
were unobtainable. We would be grateful if the appropriate people could contact us.

John Blake Publishing is an imprint of Bonnier Publishing
www.bonnierpublishing.com

CONTENTS

'The human voice is the most beautiful instrument of all but it is the most difficult to play'
RICHARD STRAUSS

FOREWORD
BY LOUIS WALSH

Yvie always credits me with changing her life. When I first met her she was spending more time singing than coaching.

I've known Yvie's husband, Gordon, for many years, and when I told him I was looking for a vocal coach for the second series of *The X Factor* in 2005, he said, 'My wife teaches singing.'

I was curious to see a photo because this person was going to be on screen, and I thought his wife might resemble him – Gordon likes his food! When he showed me this glamorous blonde, I asked for her number.

We met up a few days later and got on straight away. Yvie is funny; she likes having a laugh and doesn't take herself too seriously. Within minutes of meeting up I knew we were going to get on and I had decided I was booking her for the job. The producers of the show weren't sure because she hadn't done any TV before and this role was going to be a lot more on-screen than it was in the first series. Yvie was going to be doing Boot Camp and Judges' Houses and everything with me. That was back in the day when we didn't have the budget for huge stars to appear on Judges' Houses.

I was determined, though – I knew she was going to be good.

* * *

We were a good team: I chose the songs and told her what I wanted, and she polished the singers up. She got on well with all the singers but didn't take any nonsense from them. Her mum was a teacher, so she has that stern Scottish way of letting you know if she isn't happy, which worked well with some of the younger acts especially.

I used to watch Yvie improve the singers, and I realised that all that technical stuff she taught them really did help them to get better through the weeks. I can spot potential in singers, and Yvie really helped me bring it out of the ones who sometimes didn't have much confidence. She has more patience than me. When they used to say, 'I can't sing that song,' I would just say, 'Oh, get on with it!'

* * *

Yvie's relationship with the JLS boys was funny. I think they all fancied her a bit in a kind of Mrs Robinson way – they used to call her Miss Burnett. She milked it though – she was always tottering around in those high heels! But she didn't take any nonsense from them. She got Aston singing some great notes and all their voices became stronger and more controlled.

We both loved working with those boys: they had the right attitude because they wanted to do well. I wanted them to win but it didn't matter that they were runners-up – they had a great career because of the show.

* * *

Shayne Ward and Yvie were close.

It was her first year so she had something to prove. She worked him really hard, but he was up for that and I just knew which songs were going to get him there. I had a plan in my head from the start – I had even decided on 'Somewhere over the Rainbow' for the final.

Yvie was really excited to let me hear how Shayne was sounding in the final rehearsal. There was a bit of a silence in the studio – I think everyone knew if he sang it like that, he would win on the night.

* * *

It wasn't just the obviously good singers that Yvie helped. We had a few that needed bringing out of their shells and a few where we had to find songs that didn't show their weaknesses. We always had fun though. None more so than with Jedward and all their antics! Choreographer Brian Friedman had them jumping all over the stage but Yvie would still be nagging them about their harmonies. I think that's the key to it all: if the teaching is boring, they won't listen or work hard.

The producers ended up loving Yvie, and so did Simon Cowell and Sharon Osbourne, so she was asked to stay on and coach all the acts from then onwards.

Yvie shared my dressing room on *The X Factor*. She had more clothes and shoes than me. We would always escape in there to have a good old gossip.

If I'm at a chat show or something, she comes along and sits in the dressing room while I'm waiting around, and I sometimes take her with me as a guest for a red carpet – she loves getting dressed up.

We are genuinely great friends but I'm not biased when I say she is the best at what she does. I've witnessed it first-hand. Anyone who wants to improve their singing will get invaluable information from this book. It's about every aspect of being a singer, but Yvie tells it as it is so there will be a bit of fun in there too.

I've been in the business a long time and I've never come across anyone like Yvie. She can bring out the best in raw beginners, but she also has the ability to coach huge stars that are already established. Every singer who has worked with her loves her and gets a bit dependent on her – she is like a mother hen.

Yvie isn't perfect: she plays a lot of wrong notes on the piano, spends as much time doing her hair and make-up as the acts themselves, and if I get a gift of champagne at a show, she will usually go off home with it. But she would still be my number one choice to share a dressing room with.

Read this book, she talks a lot of sense.

Nobody does it better than Yvie Burnett.

CHAPTER ONE

ALL ABOUT ME

(AND WHY I THINK YOU COULD LEARN
FROM MY EXPERIENCE)

I must have been seven or eight and at primary school in Aberdeenshire. On one occasion, we were all told to sing 'The Twelve Days of Christmas'. Everyone else was singing in a childlike voice and then it came to me. My line was 'Five gold rings,' and I sounded like a fully-fledged opera singer. Everyone – including me – was amazed. The teacher said I had the makings of an operatic voice, not that I knew what that meant at the time.

I started listening to recordings that I found in the library by the likes of Maria Callas, Dame Joan Sutherland and Jessie Norman, and I found that whatever note they sang, I could sing too. My dad worked in the agricultural industry and my mum was a teacher, so it was a surprise to us all. No one knew where it came from.

Quite quickly – I couldn't have been more than ten

– I was asked to sing in local concerts. Lady Aberdeen, who ran the Haddo House Choral & Operatic Society (HHCOS) near to where I lived, took me under her wing. I'd stand on a box and sing solos at the same concerts in which quite big names from the world of opera, such as Dame Janet Barker, would have come up from 'Down South' to perform.

Lady Aberdeen was also very friendly with the Royal Family. I remember performing in musical plays with Prince Edward when he came to stay. We would have been around sixteen or seventeen at the time. But I was never allowed to boast. It was how you were brought up back then in north-east Scotland. That's good for life but not so good for a singer. I always wished I had more confidence when performing. To this day, singing in public always makes me nervous. Every successful singer I've worked with has this sliver of self-confidence and self-belief, no matter how nervous they are, and that's something I myself sometimes lacked.

In senior school, I was cast in all the productions. I was Dorothy in *The Wizard of Oz*, Eliza Doolittle in *My Fair Lady*, Miss Adelaide in *Guys and Dolls* and so on. But my best academic subject was languages (French and Spanish being my favourites), and I decided I wanted to become an interpreter. At the last minute, though, it was decided it would be foolish for me not to pursue the singing.

I won a place at the Royal Scottish Academy of Music and Drama (RSAMD) in Glasgow, where, of course, I was now a small fish in a big pond where everyone could sing beautifully. Most of them, what's more, had an inbuilt 'I-am-

amazing' gene. So I didn't find it a totally happy experience, although looking back, I realise I did learn a lot.

That was a three-year course followed by a further two specialising in opera as a mezzo-soprano (a voice lower than the soprano voice). Then I won a scholarship to the Guildhall School of Music & Drama in London. There were only a dozen of us on the opera course, among them the acclaimed Welsh bass-baritone, Bryn Terfel. After that came a final year at the National Opera Studio (NOS), which trains the cream of young operatic talent; I was sponsored by Glyndebourne Opera, who then gave me experience in the chorus as well as understudying solo roles.

By this stage, my confidence was growing a little and I wanted to be a soloist. I was lucky in that the Welsh National Opera had seen me perform at the National Opera Studio Showcase and invited me to sing a number of roles with them in Cardiff, such as the role of Suzuki in their acclaimed production of *Madame Butterfly*. The incredible role of Olga in Tchaikovsky's *Eugene Onegin* at Glyndebourne was followed by Offenbach's *Les Brigands* with Netherlands Opera and Wagner's *Das Rheingold* with Nantes Opera. What helped in all of this was that I was always in a costume and a wig, something I could hide behind. But if I ever did a concert dressed as me, I wasn't nearly so assured.

That mix of work continued into my thirties. By this time I was married and had two children, Emily and Ollie, who I'd take with me if I was performing somewhere, helped by a nanny or my mum, Molly. That became

'Playing the role of Lady Essex in the Opera North and Royal Opera House production of Britten's *Gloriana*.' © *Hanson*

difficult when they reached school age so I started doing a bit of teaching. My husband, Gordon, was in the music business – he signed Bros, Deacon Blue and Roachford, among many others – and I was able to tutor some of his pop and rock singers on how to get the best out of their voices.

It was Gordon who introduced me to the Irish entertainment manager Louis Walsh, who was looking for a new vocal coach for ITV's *The X Factor*. The producers had their doubts: this was an on-screen role of which I had no experience. But Louis insisted. This was 2005, the second year of the show. Louis and I did the Boot Camp together and then the Judges' House in Dublin.

One of the final three in our team was Shayne Ward.

Playing the role of Olga in two productions of Tchaikovsky's *Eugene Onegin*, at Glyndebourne Opera alongside the late Sue Chilcott as my sister Tatyana (above) and at the Welsh National Opera with Janice Watson (below, © *Catherine Ashmore*).

I worked with him on how to make his final song, 'Somewhere Over the Rainbow', really special, and I convinced him to sing higher notes than he'd ever attempted before. In opera, I was used to making the second half of a song ornate and showy. Not only did Shayne hit those notes but his brilliant performance won him the series. As a result, both Simon Cowell and Sharon Osbourne said they wanted me to coach their acts as well the following year, which was how I ended up being the *X Factor* vocal coach for all the acts. I loved it, the show became my life.

For me, Simon was always very encouraging, always knew what he wanted me to do. He never pretended he was a singing teacher, for the very good reason that he's not a singer; he left that to me. He's the sort of person you really want to please. And yes, there's an element of scariness about him because he's someone with a definite aura.

I remember on one occasion getting a text message from him at two in the morning – he often works all night – praising something I'd done with a song sung

'At my first X Factor Boot Camp in 2005 with Louis – you can spot that year's eventual winner Shayne Ward at the back along with Alexandra Burke (far right), who would later win the series in 2008.'

by Alexandra Burke. Except I didn't know it was from him because I didn't recognise the number. So I quite angrily asked whoever it was why they were texting me at that hour of the night. (This was in the days when you couldn't silence your text messages without turning off the phone.) It was a bit embarrassing when I got the reply: 'It's me. Simon.'

Sharon is one of the most generous, caring, warm individuals I've ever met. And she knows her stuff while also letting you get on with your work. I now regard her as a close friend. The first time I met her, I told her she smelled better than anyone I'd ever smelled before. She wears a particular perfume by Hermès. The next day, she handed me a bag containing a bottle of the same perfume. That turned out to be typical of her. Funnily enough, Will.i.am said how much he liked the perfume when I was first working on *The Voice UK* so I bought some for him. I'm still not sure that Will and Sharon know they smell the same!

Louis is a very special man. People poke fun at him for saying things like: 'You really made that song your own,' or 'You look like a young Gary Barlow.' His knowledge of songs is like no other. As soon as he hears the tone of someone's voice, he has the special ability to match songs to them – he's like an encyclopaedia of song. Louis is a true friend, we're constantly in touch. And he, too, is always appreciative of what you're doing.

I worked on *The X Factor* until 2010. There's no dispute that Leona Lewis, who won the show in 2006, is the best singer, and the best winner ever. She always had an incredible voice but initially didn't have the confidence to go with it. It's a terribly overused word, but the British public loved to see Leona's 'journey', the way she grew before their eyes down the weeks leading to the final. Even today, if she wants help with something, she will still phone me up to go and see her. She knows what to do on her own but she still values that extra pair of ears.

Each year, I'd be involved with *The X Factor* from August through to Christmas. In 2007, I was asked to be the vocal coach on a new programme – *Britain's Got Talent* on ITV. In that first year, Paul Potts won the show. Now there was someone with a good voice, but he needed polishing. For me he was a dream come true because he had a classical voice; however, he wanted to sing popular songs, something that became known as a crossover style of singing. So I worked with him to make his classical approach accessible to a vast TV audience.

I also coached Susan Boyle when she was famously a contestant on the show in 2009. I could tell from the off that she had a great tone and a lovely voice, but the whole package, if I can put it like that, wasn't what you'd expect. Ours became an incredibly intense, long-term relationship. For my money, her audition on the show will always be TV gold.

She'd always say to me that she wasn't clever, but that isn't true when it comes to singing. Musically, her's is an instinctive talent. Yes, she may be eccentric and yes, we now know that she has a mild form of Asperger syndrome, but she would never have become a global star if she didn't have a remarkable voice. And she has something indefinable: she can move people. I've travelled the world with her and she's mobbed wherever she goes.

All of that kept me busy up until Easter each year, but then Simon asked me to coach the singers on NBC's *America's Got Talent* before returning to the UK for the next season of *The X Factor*. I also worked with Andrew Lloyd Webber when he did the ITV talent show, *Superstar*, to find a young singer to play the title role in *Jesus Christ Superstar*.

My *annus horribilis* turned out to be 2010. I was working with Sarah Brightman in Los Angeles in March ahead of a forthcoming album and tour. And then my mum died unexpectedly back in the UK. I'm an only child so it hit me really hard. After the funeral, at which Susan Boyle sang 'Amazing Grace', she and I flew to Tokyo the very next day. On my return home, I was pitched straight into the live week of *Britain's Got Talent*, followed by *America's Got Talent* in the US.

In the middle of working on that show, I got a phone call telling me I wasn't needed on *The X Factor* that year. In the normal course of events, I'd have been upset, but I hadn't properly grieved for my mother so this tipped me over the edge – I couldn't stop crying.

When I got back to the UK, the papers were full of headlines like 'Voice Over' above stories that I'd been sacked.

Within a week, I got a call saying they wanted me back. My husband, wisely as it turned out, said I shouldn't return to the show, that I wasn't in a fit state. But I wouldn't listen to him. I went back but I wasn't myself, so I can't say I was surprised when they didn't ask me back the following year.

In time, I thought I'd better find myself something new. And then, out of the blue, I got a call from the producers of *The Voice UK*, which was about to begin on BBC1, asking if I'd like to be the resident vocal coach. I then worked on that show for five years. It was good timing because I wasn't wanted on *Britain's Got Talent*, either. Around the same time the fabulous TV show *The Big Reunion* also came along, which was fun to work on from beginning to end.

The Voice UK is more structured than *The X Factor* because the mentors – Will.i.am and so on – are also coaches. I already knew Ricky Wilson – I'd worked with him as his vocal coach as I had with Paloma Faith. I didn't know him beforehand but I've built up a real friendship with Will.i.am, the funniest, sweetest man you could ever hope to meet. He's worked with everyone from Michael Jackson to Prince and he's got incredible stories to tell.

But then I also loved working with Tom Jones. That man could have been an opera singer, he's got an amazing voice. I miss him. I also enjoyed working with Kylie – she's very knowledgeable and very good at matching the right song to the particular contestant.

This year, I worked with Gary Barlow on his BBC show, *Let It Shine*. The aim was to find five singers for his new musical, *The Band*, which is touring around the UK and then ending up in London's West End. Yet again, I loved getting to know all the contestants, and the eventual winners, Five to Five, are a really talented group of boys.

And so it continues, the excitement of finding new singing stars on TV. To me, it never becomes boring, and

'With the wonderful judges from *The Voice*.'

I'm still as thrilled as ever to be in the wings on Saturday nights while the British nation watches what we've been working on.

Funnily enough, as much as I enjoy coaching on TV, I've started singing again myself. Back in April 2016, I sang 'Caledonia' in front of 17,000 people at the Scottish Grand National in Ayr. I loved it. And, having taught so many people down the years, I realised I'd taken my own advice and learnt how to enjoy the experience. At last, I'd found a little bit of confidence myself.

It felt as though I'd come full circle.

When I look back over all these years, I wish I had known many of the things I know now when I was starting out.

That was one reason I wanted to write a book, so that I

could help people with all the vocal or emotional problems that I had. I wanted them not to feel that they were alone in their worries.

I also wanted to put pen to paper because so many people over the years have asked me to.

I've taught hundreds of people both in the UK and the US who feverishly write everything down. I joke with some of my singers who hang on my every word and tell them not to take everything I say literally!

I understand though that no matter how many lessons you have, you do forget things. Therefore it's nice to have it down in print for you to refer to.

So this is for all of you who want to start to really understand your voices, or remind yourselves of lots of things you may have learnt but forgotten. Happy reading!

CHAPTER TWO

ALL ABOUT YOU

It has taken many years of working as a singing coach for me to finally agree to write down in a book all the tips and experience I have learnt along the way. There are two types of people this book should appeal to:

- Those of you who love singing and genuinely want your voice to improve and be the best it can be, although you would never want singing to be your career.
- Those of you who want to become professional singers and need to find out what that takes.

However, this comes with a warning: if you are lazy, put this book down and go and spend your money on a couple of your favourite magazines! Proper singing takes so much more than just a good voice. On the other hand, if you think you've got the drive and determination, read on.

In these days of almost instant fame on TV, it's easy for people to think that if they sing a bit, they can become multi-millionaires by the time they are twenty. Too often, the thinking seems to be, let's not work hard at school, let's just become famous. It's a bit like a boy who is quite good at football and plays once a week with his mates thinking he will be in the Premier League by the time he's nineteen.

In both cases, these people are deluded. To make it as a top-flight footballer, you would need to be someone who spends every night after school doing their keepy-uppies and endless hours of goal practice, not the 'cool' one hanging out with their mates. Similarly, to make it as a singer, you should be practising every day. Ideally, you should also learn to play an instrument or do some sort of music class either at school or in the evenings. If that's not possible, you can listen to different types of music and read up about them so that you build up some sort of musical knowledge. You may have to miss out on a few parties because you have a rehearsal or you've got an important gig the next day and you want to look after your voice. Take note of this! In order to make it in the real world, you don't necessarily have to be the 'cool' one right now – that can come later.

So how do you become a singer and not just a person who sings?

ALL ABOUT YOU

**

Being a singer involves a psychological change in your attitude. Say, for example, you are a hairdresser: you have a good voice, and you often do karaoke at weekends to widespread acclaim from your circle of friends. You've even been asked to sing at a mate's wedding reception and you got up to sing at Christmas last year. You keep meaning to enter a talent competition but somehow you never quite manage to pluck up the courage.

If that sounds like you, here are the steps you need to take. And if it all sounds a little too far-fetched or too much like hard work, stick with what you know, whether it's hairstyling or another career path! But if you are serious in your ambition to sing, now's the time to book a consultation with a vocal coach or singing teacher. They will give you an unbiased opinion as to whether or not you have potential. (Your mates, after a few beers, might not be the best judges...)

Don't tell me you can't afford a lesson (someone local shouldn't be expensive for one lesson at least). Naturally, the price might depend on where you live in the country.

If you really want this, don't go out this weekend and instead put the money in a pot for the lesson. Alternatively, get all your mates and relatives who think you're good to donate £1 each towards the lesson. Tell them they are investing in your future career as a singer and now let's see if they really do believe you can make it. If £1 is beyond them, I have my worries!

OK, let's assume you have your consultation booked

and the money to pay for it ready. Now find a backing track on the Internet of a song you think shows your voice off to its best advantage.

Tell the teacher when you get there that you're thinking of making singing your career and you want an honest opinion on whether you have the potential to make it or not. OK, so this is just one opinion, and you can still ignore it or go for a second opinion, but the most important thing is you have taken the first step towards taking singing seriously.

Let's assume the teacher says you have a good voice but it needs work and it all depends how dedicated you are. If your reaction is 'I don't know how dedicated I am', another career is calling you. But, on the other hand, if your immediate reaction is 'Yes! He or she didn't laugh at my efforts and say it wasn't possible!' then you are on your way.

So, read on... let's get to work!

Proper singers are like athletes (I apologise in advance for the number of times I will repeat this). There are many muscles working the larynx (voice box), and these muscles need to be exercised and looked after properly to avoid damage or injury.

As a general rule there are two types of famous singer. The first is the one who learnt basic singing technique at a young age and kept learning along the way, often with the help of a coach.

Let's liken a singing coach to a tennis coach. For example, Andy Murray can play tennis, and he's been the world's number one player. So why would he need a coach? The answer is that whether in sport or singing, the role of a coach is to help with technique, which can improve performance and keep the muscles safe from injury. Even if you are at the top of your game, you always need a coach to help you avoid slipping into bad habits, which can inhibit the way you perform or cause unnecessary tension, which can lead to injury.

The second type of singer is the one who has made it big because they are a great songwriter or have sung great songs, not necessarily because they are a great singer. Some people love their voices; their voices will be unique and incredible in their own way, and they may have a great tone, but not such a great technique. To me many of these singers sound like their voices are damaged. I'm thinking of the likes of Bob Dylan, the late Leonard Cohen or Bonnie Tyler. I wouldn't choose to listen to these voices personally, but I understand why people do and they have incredible songs.

Many singers who haven't worked on technique will eventually have vocal problems, because the workload is too much without learning ways to build up stamina and not to strain the voice. Often they realise straight away that they need a coach and avoid any vocal damage, but more frequently it's only when they lose their voices on a huge arena or stadium tour that a coach or even a surgeon is called in. The sad thing is that many singers think a coach will change the unique way they sound, but in many cases they won't, they will just make their technique safer. It often turns out OK in the end for this second type of singer, because by that stage in their career they can afford to have a coach flown in to be there for them and to address whatever the problem is. However, so many singers in this situation have confided in me, 'If only I had known all this technical stuff at the start of my career…'

So, here you are. You are either at the start of your career reading this book or you are in the middle of your singing career and recognise that you need a bit of help.

It's really important to understand that as singers we are always learning and we never know it all. Our voices change all the time, whether with age or just with the way we are using them, and so we always need to be one step ahead of these changes.

In fact our voices can sound and feel different on a daily basis, whether that's due to tiredness, illness, emotion (for example, having argued with your partner the night before), a bad acoustic in the venue of your gig or just your frame of mind on a particular day. Technique is about helping you to be more consistent and able to deal with whatever 'voice' you have that day. If you don't learn to understand how your voice does what it does, you can never learn to be consistent. Of course there are always exceptions. There are people who never sing too high, never too loud and never have any major problems. They just sing the way they sing and everything works out fine for them. But they are the lucky few and the rest of us need to make sure we are as good as we can be.

So, turn the page and let's move on to understanding your God-given instrument and welcome in a bit of hard work!

CHAPTER THREE

THE SINGER'S RULEBOOK

WHY YOU SHOULD LOOK AFTER YOUR VOICE – AND HOW TO GO ABOUT IT

All right, so you have decided: You are not someone who sings a bit; you are now a singer!

Once you take that momentous step, here is the way you absolutely have to live your life. There are no alternatives, no half measures: it's all or nothing.

We singing teachers often refer to keeping the voice healthy as 'vocal hygiene'. Looking after your voice, in the ways we are going to discuss, must become second nature to you. After years of working as an opera singer, I wouldn't dream of doing anything that would damage my voice in any way, whether temporarily or permanently.

Why wouldn't any type of professional singer feel the same way?

Pop and rock singers are thought to have a very cool job, and being sensible isn't considered cool. Professional athletes are still thought of as cool, though, and they are extremely disciplined. If you think of yourself as a rock star who has to flout authority and be a bad boy (or girl), think again. That's your public persona. In private, many rock stars are not quite as wild as they would have you believe. I know a few who exercise their voices every day so don't be deceived. Have a read of what Alexandra Burke has to say, for example, in Chapter Four (page 33) about the difference between her public and private personas.

So here's the rulebook:

Rule One: You NEVER Shout

If you are a football fan, you smile, you clap, you jump up and down… but you DO NOT shout. If you are in a club and the music is so loud that you can't speak without shouting, then speak into your friend's ear or take them away from the music to talk to them. Even write notes in your phone, if necessary. They can laugh all they like but you are a singer, you NEVER shout.

To sum up: try not to raise your voice if you are a singer, unless you have kids or a particularly annoying partner!

> **Tip**
> When music is so loud that you have to shout above it to be heard, speak in a well-articulated, slightly higher-pitched way. That way, your voice will be more resonant so it will carry more, and you will be heard better without so much strain.

Rule Two: If You Smoke, You're a Fool

Hot burning smoke passing across your vocal folds is never a good idea. Tar filling up your lungs, making you out of breath? That's crazy. Going outside in the cold for a cheeky cigarette and catching a chill is pretty stupid too. And as for developing a smoker's cough which aggravates your voice... well, you don't need me to tell you why that isn't good news.

However, if you're a singer who smokes and you are already performing regularly, you can give up smoking gradually. It's a good idea to consult your GP to get some help with this. You will find when you give up smoking that lots of phlegm appears (it's the body's way of getting rid of mucus as it detoxifies), and it will take about six weeks before your voice goes back to normal. It may well get worse before it gets better, but in the long run you will see and feel a big improvement.

'OK,' I hear you telling me, 'There are singers who smoke and they sound great. Don't be such an old nag!'

Fine, carry on: it's your health, it's your voice. All I'm saying is that if you give up, you will have more range, better breathing techniques, less cracking and more stamina. It's your life, you choose!

To sum up: unless you like smelling like an old ashtray, give up smoking NOW! You could spend the money you save on singing lessons.

Rule Three: If You Have a Sore Throat and You Don't Have to Perform, Cancel Your Gig

Singing on an infection is possible but never ideal. However, those of us who make a living as a singer know that if we cancel, we don't get paid. So if cancelling isn't an option, make sure you get plenty of rest before and after the gig.

The type of sore throat, cold or infection you can and cannot sing on is something you learn over the years as a singer, but for beginners and those of you who are still a little unsure, here are some general guidelines:

- If it hurts a bit, you think it's an infection rather than soreness because you have strained your voice (it should NEVER hurt to sing), and your voice sounds the way it normally does, then you will probably be all right if you absolutely have to do the gig so that you don't let people down.
- If you have a cold that makes you sound nasal but all your usual notes are there, it's probably a head cold and you are OK to sing. But try to do less than usual if possible and stop if your voice starts to go.
- If you have laryngitis (a sign of this is your singing or speaking voice cutting out), DO NOT SING! You could do yourself permanent damage. If you only have a couple of lines to sing or it is unavoidable, then do the bare minimum with extreme caution, but more than that is extremely dangerous. You will sound pretty bad anyway so you won't be doing your reputation much good.

- If you have a bad cold which is causing you to cough, has gone to your chest and parts of your voice, or is stopping certain notes from coming out, DO NOT SING! Again, this is risking permanent damage, so always weigh up the risks against your desire to do the gig and err on the safe side. Cancelling one gig rather than risking having to cancel for weeks is surely the safer option. If you are in any doubt whatsoever, seek medical advice!

Singing should never hurt. Yes, singing can sometimes make your voice feel tired, but one of the aims of this book is to help you build up your stamina.

Here's what to do if you get ill:

- If you can go to bed and sleep it off, please do so. When we rest, our body heals itself. Getting stressed about not being able to sing will only make it worse.
- If it's a cold, fill a bowl with boiling water, put a towel over your head and breathe in the steam. This should help shift the mucus. Don't be tempted to add fancy menthol products or the like to the water – the steam alone is enough.
- If you have a throat infection, gargle with some salt dissolved in hot water. Here, I'm talking about a very small amount of salt, maybe half a teaspoon to a large glass of hot water. Don't use too much as it may cause irritation. I always do this at the first sign of soreness because it feels like I'm disinfecting my throat and killing germs.

- Always drink plenty of liquid to flush out any germs from your system. Health experts recommend 2 litres of water per day; that works for singers too.

A recent conversation with X *Factor* runner-up Olly Murs reminded me how much I nag my students about what to do when they are ill. Olly quoted me, word for word, telling him to hum a little to get his voice back gradually and to steam when he could. He also reminded me that I said to drink pineapple juice (fresh pineapple juice is best if you can get it). Unlike orange juice, pineapple doesn't seem to cause acid reflux and it makes a dry mouth feel better. For more of its benefits, see page 29. It's a good job my students remember what I teach them because often I forget my own tips myself!

The main thing to try and avoid is coughing. Sometimes during the night we get a coughing fit when we have a cold, because all the resulting mucus runs onto our vocal folds while we are lying down. Sit up at once, suck a pastille or sip a glass of water and breathe, but make sure you have finished your pastille before you go back to sleep – I don't want you choking! I recommend my singers to use glycerine pastilles and find Grether's are excellent.

You can try and stop the cough in the first place by doing a series of deep breaths with an open throat like the start of a yawn. Do this for a few minutes until you feel calm, then try to sleep again. If you start coughing again, repeat the whole process.

Coughing can damage the vocal folds so we need to avoid it if we possibly can.

If you're at all worried that your voice might have been damaged through singing on an infection, don't panic. It can sometimes take a couple of weeks for it to return to normal – after a bad cough, for example. However, if after a few weeks there is no improvement, ask your GP to refer you to a laryngologist (a throat specialist). It may be necessary to pay for this privately, but as a singer nothing is more important than the health of your voice.

To sum up: if you use your voice when you are unwell then you can damage it, so be careful.

Would Wayne Rooney play with a sore foot? Nah, he'd put his feet up and watch the match on TV!

Rule Four: Avoid Foods That Can Cause Vocal Problems

Many foods are problematic for singers. However, everyone reacts differently and to varying degrees. You will get to know your own voice and how resilient or sensitive it is.

I have worked with many singers who have major problems with certain foods, but I have also sung in France, where having a glass of red wine before a performance is normal practice. You really have to rely on your own common sense, but here are some guidelines.

The main food-related problem for singers is acid reflux. This is a burning sensation often known as heartburn, caused by stomach acid flowing back up into the food pipe. The main causes are as follows:

- Acidic foods (e.g. tomatoes or orange juice)
- Spicy foods (e.g. curries, onions, chillies and so on)

- Fizzy drinks
- Alcohol
- Fried or greasy foods
- Smoking
- Eating late

The symptoms of acid reflux are as follows:

- A burning sensation in the back of the throat
- Mucus that you constantly have to clear from the back of the throat, which can make you crack notes or cough
- A morning cough

CURES FOR ACID REFLUX

- Place a big book under the top part of your mattress so that you always sleep slightly upright. I'm talking about an enormous hardback novel or an encyclopedia (pop to your local charity shop to pick one up cheaply, if you don't have one to hand).
- Do not eat late at night, because the food will not be properly digested and when you are lying down/ sleeping, the digestive acid from your stomach will travel upwards and onto the oesophagus which will then cause irritation to your vocal folds. Keep upright (sitting or standing) for a few hours after you eat. Ideally you should leave three hours for food to digest before you go to bed.
- Cut out foods which affect you in this way.

Other foods that can cause problems for singers are as follows:

- Dairy products, especially milk, cheese, cream and ice cream, which can create mucus. Mucus prevents the voice from coming out clearly because it can sit on or around the vocal folds and often causes us to cough or clear our throats, which can irritate the vocal folds.
- Chocolate (including hot chocolate, chocolate biscuits and chocolate cake). It's a no-no for singers, especially just before a performance. Obviously if you are singing on Saturday night then you can have a bar of chocolate on Thursday evening – just use common sense. As a general rule, chocolate clogs up the vocal folds with mucus so it is best avoided.

To sum up: EAT LIKE A SINGER.

The exception for me is when I feel a cold coming on, I head for my favourite Thai restaurant and enjoy a very hot chilli soup. I swear by that soup, I'm convinced it stops a cold in its tracks. Sometimes I do break my own rules!

Rule Five: Always Keep the Larynx at an Even Temperature

I suggest wearing a scarf when it's cold and covering your mouth and nose in very frosty weather because we are more susceptible to infections and colds when exposed to extreme changes of temperature. Also, the insides of our noses getting cold makes it easier for the rhinovirus (the predominant cause of the common cold) to breed. Researchers have found that rhinoviruses reproduce more efficiently in the cooler temperatures found inside the nose, which is why we always need to wear scarves over them.

Rule Six: Keep Hydrated

Make it a rule never to get dehydrated as a singer. It takes around five hours to hydrate the vocal folds, so start drinking as soon as you wake up. There is no point in not drinking all day and then downing two pints of water ten minutes before your gig. Keep hydrated all day!

CAUSES OF DEHYDRATION

- Medication
  Examples are antihistamines and sinus medications but there are many others. If you get hay fever and take antihistamines, you may have to drink more water to compensate for the drying effect the tablets might have. As always, it is best to get your GP's advice on this.

- Caffeine
  Fizzy drinks, coffee, tea, cola and many energy drinks all contain caffeine, which dehydrates. Just drink them in moderation.

- Air conditioning
  If at all possible, ask for air conditioning to be switched off. If you have to put up with it – on a plane, for example – drink plenty of water to compensate.
  To sum up: KEEP HYDRATED. Drink water until your pee is very pale!

Hydrating tip

Pineapple juice is great for keeping your thirst quenched. If you are feeling thirsty with nerves (for example, just before an audition or a performance), pineapple juice makes you feel less dry than water alone. It contains an enzyme with anti-inflammatory properties and is also thought to help disrupt the horrible mucus we get when we have a cough or cold. I recommend my students use it when they are unwell instead of cough mixture. Its properties may not be proven but it certainly seems to benefit lots of my singers.

Often, when I'm with my singers at an important gig or a TV show, we'll do a really good warm-up and then just before they go on, they'll say, 'Yvie, did you bring pineapple juice?' Of course I did!

Rule Seven: Be Careful with Alcohol

Alcohol dehydrates, so don't drink it on the day of a gig; don't drink the night before either, because you will start the day with less energy and be more dehydrated. Having a quick glass to make you feel confident is a no-no. You will think you sound better, but it will dry your voice out and you won't sound as good as you think you do.

Remember, if it affects your ability to drive, it also

affects your ability to sing. Generally, too much alcohol on a regular basis isn't a good idea for a singer – or anyone else for that matter!

After a late night drinking, we all wake up with a croaky throat. When we start talking, it sounds an octave lower than usual! Once in a blue moon is all right, but if you do this every week and constantly sing on a croaky throat, that's when you risk damaging your voice. It's not acting like a SINGER, is it?

Being a singer means singing is your priority. If you don't have to sing the next day, that's fine, but occasionally you will have to make a sacrifice and stick to water.

To sum up: many of us like a drink, but just remember you are now a SINGER!

Rule Eight: Constant Exercise

Imagine you are a professional athlete. Your training is so important that you may spend many months exercising at high altitude to get your body used to having less oxygen. You may have to do endless weeks of fitness boot camps and pushing yourself to an extreme level. Every day you train and you're obsessive about it, even on holiday. It should be the same for a professional singer, because if you miss more than a day of exercising your voice, your muscles will get lazy.

Now I'm not expecting you to spend hours while you are on holiday practising scales, but fifteen minutes per day, every day, is essential. You will find that the more regularly your voice is exercised, the better it works.

If you are a bit under the weather or excessively tired,

just hum a little or have one day, but only one, of total rest. However, if you have a sore throat, a bad cold or laryngitis, then you MUST NOT sing, so only then can you have time off from your normal regime.

Don't talk either: talking can be just as tiring as singing, sometimes more so.

It's worth noting here that whispering is actually worse than talking. You will put your voice under more strain if you whisper, so get yourself a notebook and a pen! As soon as you feel a bit better, it's important to start humming a little bit just to get the muscles working again.

Of course, if you have strained your voice at a gig and it feels sore or heavy, have one day of vocal rest; the next day, if it feels better, start humming gently. The vicious cycle of 'strain your voice, go on vocal rest, strain your voice again' is something to be avoided.

I find myself getting increasingly frustrated when I see singers on the day of a gig or a TV show holding up signs that say, 'I'm on vocal rest.' You should never be straining your voice to that extent and then thinking that vocal rest will fix all problems. Of course, vocal rest can be a good thing – we need it occasionally when we are tired or ill. But there is no substitute for learning good technique so that you don't strain in the first place. That's the aim of this book! However, if you are in any doubt, please do go and see your GP.

I have had many strange looks while singing a few scales on holiday, but if you need to sing at a gig as soon as you get back home then you must keep your voice in peak condition. Remember, your vocal stamina improves when you sing every day. You will notice that after time off, your voice tires more easily.

To sum up: if you can't find fifteen minutes a day to sing then I don't know how you have managed to read this far into the book.

It's your JOB, stop making excuses!

> **Holiday tip**
> You can often find a piano in the ballroom or maybe the bar of a hotel, and you can always sneak in there in the mornings to do a few scales – with permission from the hotel staff of course!

Rule Nine: Always Warm Up

NEVER EVER sing without first warming your voice up, otherwise you can cause strain. You will always sing better anyway once you have warmed up.

If you don't know how to warm up, even humming or just singing a song gently will help. There is, however, a warming-up chapter later in the book (see pages 73–89).

After a very tiring gig, you should always warm down a bit too, which we will also discuss later in Chapter 7, page 87.

These, then, are the rules – they are all common sense really.

I know I say this until I'm blue in the face but... THINK OF YOURSELF AS AN ATHLETE AND ALWAYS TAKE CARE OF YOURSELF AND YOUR VOICE!

CHAPTER FOUR

TAKE A TIP FROM THE STARS

HOW FAMOUS FACES LOOK AFTER FAMOUS VOICES

As I keep on telling you, your most precious instrument is your voice, and no one knows this more than the following collection of star singers, each of them at the top of their game. But none of them would stay there for long if they abused their voice. So here's what they have to say...

Michael Ball – singer, actor and broadcaster

'I've never had singing lessons but I seem to have worked out my own technique over the years. I tend to have a dry mouth when I step out on stage so I tuck a Vocalzone [a type of throat lozenge] into my cheek and it stays there throughout the performance!'

Gary Barlow – singer, songwriter and frontman of Take That

'My tips for keeping my vocals up to scratch on tour are to turn off the air con and open the windows, don't talk too loudly during the day and also avoid dairy food. Do a light warm up in the mid-afternoon, and then do a full warm up forty-five minutes before the show. Don't get overexcited during the show and over sing (so that you're shouting), and keep it cool. Finally, sleep, sleep and more sleep!'

Susan Boyle – *Britain's Got Talent* runner-up in 2009

'I don't drink alcohol and I try to drink as much water as I can. If I have a performance coming up, I try to avoid dairy products. If I have milk, it will be skimmed or lactose-free.'

Alexandra Burke – *The X Factor* winner in 2008

'If I get a sore throat, the first thing I do is stop talking. I also invested in an amazing steamer. I don't use it every day, but if I'm feeling a bit run down or my voice is tired, I'll heat up some water and breathe in the steam. I also swear by a liquorice-based tea called Throat Coat, which

I drink every single day. And if my voice is sounding like Barry White's, I'll chomp on raw ginger about an hour and a half before a performance, maybe for about five minutes before swallowing it. I exercise between three and four times a week, which includes running on a treadmill and singing at the same time. That will increase your vocal stamina. I never touch alcohol if I'm going to be performing and I always try and get eight hours' sleep a night.'

Ben Forster – *Superstar* winner in 2012

'I played the title role in *The Phantom of the Opera* for twenty months in the West End and I never socialised after the show and I never drank alcohol if I was going to be singing the following day. I always warm up with vocal exercises before any performance and then warm down afterwards, something I learnt at college. Also, I'll have a vocal massage once every week or so. They massage my vocal muscles and my larynx and move my voice box around. And I'll give myself a regular nasal douche, which involves putting a saline solution in one nostril, which then travels down the other nostril. It sounds pretty unpleasant but it keeps infections at bay, as well as keeping you hydrated.'

TJ Jackson – member of boy band 3T and nephew of the late great Michael Jackson

'I do a lot of mimicking sounds and voices. I've found it gives me a way to add some flexibility to my voice and helps keep it challenged and solid. Like a parrot, I will repeat anything I hear – from a siren going off to a baby crying – and harmonise with it. It all helps with controlling and improving your voice.

'It's important to warm up your voice before you're going to sing. Like any muscle, it's best to get it ready to perform and to protect it from injury. I'm not a tea drinker so I usually just drink a cup of hot water right before I'm about to warm up.

'Whenever I have to take a flight, I'm really big on staying hydrated. If I don't drink a lot of water, I get dehydrated easily, especially in my throat. And, when dehydrated, my voice feels vulnerable and weak. It makes singing so much more difficult, even painful at times. So I try to avoid dehydration at all costs. And I don't just start on the flight – I usually start the day beforehand by drinking lots of water.

'My uncle Michael was huge on warming up. I remember being a young kid travelling with him overseas, and if he ever had a performance, he'd call his vocal coach to warm him up. He could be in Asia or Europe and still, he'd call back to Los Angeles so that he could properly prepare his voice for a show. And remember, this was before video chats and smartphones, so some planning needed to be done. But he'd get it done. They'd do all types of exercises for what seemed like forever, but he was adamant about being ready to go and in perfect condition for a performance. I've taken that lesson with me and still to this day do exercises before a session or performance. That's non-negotiable as I want to preserve my voice and prepare it properly.'

Aled Jones – singer, presenter and actor

'I'm very lucky that I've been blessed with a strong voice. I've only ever had to cancel a handful of concerts throughout my entire career. Unlike some singers, I can have a cup of tea with milk before a concert, although not any chocolate, of course. I might take glycerine tablets to lubricate my voice but that's about it. If I'm touring, I'll sing more and more each day before it begins just to get the muscle used to singing again. And I do sing around the house, especially if I'm learning a new song. But then my daughter and son sing a lot, too, although we're not quite the von Trapp family!'

Myleene Klass – singer (Hear'Say), pianist, model and TV and radio presenter

'You're a machine. Your voice box, your diaphragm, your lungs, your body... you are the instrument. And you have to take care of it. So, don't ever think you can be a passenger. Get the right amount of sleep and it will be worth it. If someone gives you a job you absolutely love, it's not a job at all: it's a privilege. So don't abuse it. If I do get a croaky throat, I reach for a hot toddy – whisky, lemon and boiling water. And I'm a big fan of a steamer. Get your head under a towel and let the steam do its work.'

Leona Lewis – *The X Factor* winner in 2006

'How do I look after my voice? One of my favourite exercises is tongue trills. It's a nice gentle way to warm up the voice at any time of day or night – and it really makes a difference.'

Joe McElderry – *The X Factor* winner in 2009

'I know my limits vocally – I don't drink a lot of alcohol when I'm on tour. Your voice is an instrument. As someone once said to me, you wouldn't go and pour red wine over an electric piano. You can't party until three in the morning and then do two shows the next day. Of course, I sometimes get a sore throat.

'Someone gave me a great tip a few years ago: try gargling occasionally with bicarbonate of soda and water. I'll also use good old honey and lemon. But at all times,

I drink lots of water, which keeps your larynx and your body hydrated. I always do a warm-up before every show: up and down the scales to get your jaw moving and all the muscles in your face working properly. And I'll try and do a half-hour physical workout.'

Dannii Minogue – singer, dancer, songwriter, model, actress and TV judge

'The two things that I find mess with the voice the most are lack of sleep and talking in loud environments. Performers who want to sing with clarity and energy sometimes have to go to bed at odd hours, just to get enough sleep. A nap is always a great idea on show day, even if it's just ten minutes of resting. And try to avoid noisy parties or restaurants if you feel you're running low.'

Lucy O'Byrne – Runner-up on *The Voice UK* and West End performer

'My main tip for vocal maintenance is just treat it [your voice] with respect. I've learnt that a lot in the last few months particularly while performing in *Les Misérables*. Don't just assume it will always be there.

'If you want it to be your future, take it seriously. You don't need to be one of those people that spend their life permanently attached to a steam inhaler, but warm up properly, drink enough water, get enough vocal rest on your days off and don't go out the night before a show. Also, I drink a lot of ginger tea during the day and turmeric tea after a show – it's a natural powerful anti-inflammatory.'

Paul Potts – *Britain's Got Talent* winner in 2007

'When it comes to throat problems, prevention is better than cure. Remember that your larynx is a muscle like any other and needs to be warmed up and down. Make sure you drink plenty of fluids, preferably water. Colds are difficult to fight against, but always try to get enough rest to prevent catching a cold in the first place. Support your immune system by making sure you have enough antioxidants from fruit and vegetables. I like to have a supply of echinacea around if family members have a cold so I can dose myself up.

'Even so, there's always a risk that a cold will find its way through and then you need to manage your throat. Don't overload it by singing too much and try to manage any cough. Honey and lemon can help soothe the throat and free it from catarrh. If you feel any pain in your throat while performing, then you should rest your voice as much as you can. Get into a steam room if possible, or put your face over a bowl of steaming hot water with a towel over your head as this will help keep your larynx moist. A gargle with honey and lemon won't harm your voice at all.'

Kevin Simm – former member of Liberty X, *The Voice UK* winner in 2016

'If you look after your body, you shouldn't have too much trouble with your voice. I'm pretty fit, but then I go running on the open road up to four times a week, up to two hours a time. I always run to music and it's usually hip hop, not the sort of songs I sing myself. If I've got a show coming up, I try to get as much rest as possible. But if I do catch a cold, I'll drink as much liquid as possible and sleep for as long as I can. And then choose the songs that are the least demanding!'

Shayne Ward – *The X Factor* winner in 2005

'I've had a few scares with my voice. The very night I won X Factor, I sang at G-A-Y, a famous club in London, and then was interviewed on the GMTV sofa the next morning. I'd overdone it. In fact, I remember coming off stage at G-A-Y and it was as if something had clicked at the back of my throat.

'When I was in America recording my first album I had to have surgery to remove nodules on my vocal cords. I asked the surgeon whether the operation would be successful and he didn't mince his words. He couldn't put it higher, he said, than fifty-fifty. Luckily, it worked out for me.

'One of the reasons for that, I've always believed, is as a direct result of Yvie teaching me to warm up my voice before a performance and warm it down afterwards. That attention to detail meant I was in much better shape than I otherwise might have been. And it's something I continue to do to this day. If I do ever get a cold, I always use a steamer and try not to talk wherever possible until my voice feels strong again.'

Ricky Wilson – frontman of Kaiser Chiefs and former judge on *The Voice UK*

'If you do lose your voice, and it's going to happen at some point, the worst thing is to worry about it. Sleepless nights and panic don't bring voices back. I have my own rituals although they'd be useless to anyone else but me. Of course, I warm up my voice but mostly this is a distraction building up to a performance. I find the key is having my own dressing room – that's what I tell the others, at any rate! Find what works best for you, but that can take years. Oh, and don't go to the after-party.'

Finally, I've told you a number of times that singers should think like athletes! Here is a world-famous athlete turned commentator with some insight into how he looks after one of the most famous voices in British sport...

Brendan Foster CBE – former long-distance runner, athletics commentator and founder of the Great North Run

'I have a nasal voice and a Geordie accent but if I'd had training and elocution lessons I probably wouldn't have lasted a week. It's probably that distinctive unconventional sound that I have that somehow works!

'Of course to sustain a career as a professional voice user whether as a singer or a commentator you have to be disciplined. Whatever style or accent you've got you have to learn your craft, have the knowledge and always prepare or train.

'Sometimes at a major [athletics] event I might be commentating for ten days in succession, and in the case of a marathon, I'm talking for 5 hours continuously without a break. You need to be prepared for that. You have to give up alcohol and exercise by running or walking every day. In other words, you have to treat the job like an athlete would.

'Maybe I'm lucky that having been an athlete I was used to being disciplined so I haven't had any problems keeping to the same rules.'

CHAPTER FIVE

TECHNIQUE EXPLAINED

Before going into detail in the other chapters of this book about how to work on your voice and vocal technique, I need to explain exactly the technique I am going to teach you and what it will consist of. To understand this, I must take you back to how and where I have learnt what I know and which bits of this knowledge I need to impart to you.

My purpose when writing this book was to offer the singer a textbook that is understandable, to the point and informative. For years, I have searched the shelves of many music shops for books about singing. There are some great ones out there, but they are mainly for people who already have an understanding of vocal technique or for singing teachers. Almost all those I have read needed the reader to be highly intelligent to the point of being superhuman. The reader would have to read and re-read and be willing to study terminology which is beyond me in many cases and therefore (I would assume) baffling to a beginner. Even as a professional opera singer with a degree in music, I've struggled to get past the first chapters of many of these books without needing a lie down! However, I do understand why so many people who write singing books make them incredibly detailed and complicated, as it is the way we are all encouraged to teach now.

It is normal nowadays for students to understand so much detail as far as the complexities of the voice and the vocal mechanism are concerned, but in my opinion this expectation of all singers to know every name of every muscle and cartilage, and their functions, can sometimes cause over-thinking and tension from worrying that they are doing everything correctly. I believe that in many cases, this can detract from natural singing and hinder performance rather than improve it. If they learn solely from a book that is far too complicated, a singer may not be able to get back to their natural instincts due to too much scary detail that they don't understand being thrown at them.

When I first started singing, before many of you who are reading this book were born (yes, I'm fairly ancient!), singing lessons were quite often based primarily on imagery. For example, one teacher used to tell students to imagine a flower, another said to imagine a keyboard on their forehead so that the sound came out from there, and one eminent teacher even told students to imagine the colour orange. In conjunction with this, we would be shown the locations of the various muscles we needed to use, but not in so much detail that it put us off or confused us. We certainly didn't learn the name of each one – we just spent a lot of time singing. I remember being taught lots of technique, but it was a bit hit-and-miss as to whether we were on the same wavelength as our teacher and whether we could imagine the same things as them – the imagery didn't always make sense. However, things were developing in the singing world around that time, and many teachers were adding much more detailed explanations of the vocal anatomy and mechanism to their lessons.

By then I was working as a professional opera soloist, and thankfully I had built up a solid technique of my own, so finding out all the new techniques based more on fact and knowledge of vocal anatomy rather than pure imagery was fascinating and added to what I already knew. This helped me to understand my voice more and more over the years, and as I understood more, I became more confident in my ability to teach others. It is still necessary to use imagery because we can't actually see our voices in the way that piano players or violinists can visualise their instruments. That said, imagery works best in conjunction with facts.

So what I'm really saying is that it's good to have as much knowledge as you can but not be bombarded with it from the start. You must not feel inadequate if you find learning about vocal technique a bit overwhelming. What I also need to stress is that I'm still constantly learning and updating my beliefs and thoughts, although my core technical basis remains solid.

Good singing teachers don't just stick to one thing and think they know it all. I have read papers from many eminent singing teachers throughout the world, whose teaching is still evolving, albeit by small details. They feel that they never stop learning, and in my opinion that's what makes them great teachers.

And so back to what I aim to teach you in this book. Any words I use which you don't understand will be explained in the chapters that follow, and there is also a glossary of the main words and phrases at the end of the book (see pages 247–254).

The basis of my technique is 'bel canto'. This is a traditional opera method, which literally means 'beautiful singing' in Italian. However, although the name sounds simple, the technique involves much hard work and commitment. The singer is first taught diaphragmatic breathing and support. In conjunction with this, the voice is trained in a way that exercises it through a series of vocalises and scales. Usually the teacher begins with perfecting one note on a series of vowels until the student can move on to more complicated phrases. The desired result is a voice without obvious 'breaks' that can move with ease up and down the range. Any volume or dynamics needed can be achieved even within one note.

The result of this is a technique so polished and practised that when singing a song, it becomes so automatic and consistent that the singer can totally focus on the meaning of the words and the passion and artistic excellence of their performance.

TECHNIQUE EXPLAINED

In a nutshell, what this means for all the singers I work with, regardless of style (musical theatre, pop, rock, jazz, classical etc.), is that they learn the same basic core principles of technique and then have the freedom of a solid base which they can colour with whatever style they want. Additional contemporary or stylistic skills can be added when needed.

You will still sound like you, but your voice will be safer from injury. You will have more control, more range and more stamina, and on account of all that, you will hopefully have so much more confidence. However, as I have already mentioned, I have added to my 'bel canto' technique with a few things picked up over the years.

There are many good vocal techniques out there, but in my opinion not one of them can stand alone like 'bel canto', although they have an important place in the singing world and much can be learnt from them. I'm not going to single any technique out because I don't believe in them sufficiently to bring them to your attention, but if you are already studying one such technique, please remember that it is not the be-all and end-all of singing: always keep an open mind.

Some of you reading this might be religious. The majority of us believe in something, but there is a big difference between a religion and a cult. My advice would be, if it seems like your teacher is too set on one 'cult-like' technique, step away a bit every now and then and broaden your horizons – your voice will thank you for it. Maybe read up about other techniques, talk to other singers or have a one-off consultation with someone who teaches differently. If your technique works for you, that's fine, but often people come to me saying, 'I've been unsure of everything I've been doing for a while.'

Faddy singing techniques are like faddy diets. Although you may be one of the people for whom the latest diet craze is life-changing, most people will do better sticking to the simple 'eat less, exercise more' regime. Just because it's fashionable it doesn't mean it's good. There's no point in 'changing it up' or making it more 'on trend' – singing technique doesn't follow fashion.

In the same way, doctors learn new methods of treating patients, which add to their overall knowledge, but they don't take away from the fundamental learning they have relied on to treat patients for centuries. What I have learnt most of all over the years is that just because someone is a good singer it doesn't mean they are necessarily a good teacher.

In the beginning, my voice was hard to control and I had problems mastering technique, so I understand singers' problems. If the teacher has always found it easy then they will struggle to fix things you find difficult. And if other singers find it all easy while you struggle, don't worry about it. All voices take different amounts of time to become technically secure.

Just as Andy Murray is still working on and improving his technique after all his success, great singers constantly work on perfection too. So what we are going to work on here is giving you an understanding of how your whole body and the correct use of certain muscles will improve your voice and give you the ability to do all the things you want to do with it. Correct posture is vital, especially in the learning stages, and an understanding of correct breathing in order to support your voice will be where you will see the greatest improvement. How you are feeling greatly affects your voice as well, so we will look at how to build your confidence and control your mind in the correct way. Emotions can really impact your performance; it's great to see an emotional performance, but equally if you aren't feeling well emotionally, your voice can suffer. It's important to see this and find a way to deal with it.

Warming up is an important part of your daily routine. It doesn't need to be complicated and should be geared to suit your own voice. It's better to make up an easy personal routine than switch on a random generic warm-up that may not be right for you, and so I will show you what to do.

Daily practice sessions are vital in order to exercise the voice in the correct way. You will learn how to practise properly, because practising wrongly for hours can do untold damage. For those of you who are beginners, we will work on how to learn a song, and it won't hurt to revisit the basics if you happen to be a professional singer reading this book. As I will repeat ad infinitum, we are always learning. Auditioning techniques will be explored and we will gain some tips from some of the music industry's biggest stars. And if you need to find a singing teacher, I will help you decide how to find the right one for you.

Once you have learnt all this, you will need to know how to get into the business – and what's more, how to SURVIVE in it – and so we can explore some ideas about that.

So, let's get started. Here are some of the main reasons people want to learn vocal technique:

My Throat Hurts When I Sing

This should NEVER happen. You can feel tired, and sometimes after a very big gig, your voice or throat will feel what I call 'heavy'. When this is the case, I will give you tips on how to deal with that, but it should NEVER hurt.

I Lose Stamina After a Couple of Songs and Want to Be Able to Sing for Longer

Vocal technique will completely sort this out. It's about practising properly – a bit like someone who struggles to run for the bus eventually learning how to run a marathon.

I Can't Reach the High Notes

Vocal technique will definitely help you increase your range, but some people are lower singers than others – you just need to find songs in your key or change the songs you like into a key to suit you.

I Run Out of Breath in the Middle of a Phrase

You can learn to breathe properly and it will change your life – well, your SINGING life anyway! See the chapter that follows (page 57).

Nerves Make My Voice Wobble

Working on breathing and how to support your voice will mean that even when you are shaking from head to toe, you can trick everyone into thinking you are super-confident because your voice will be totally controlled.

One Day I'm Great, the Next I Sound Rubbish

Consistency is something that comes from a good technique. In fact, it's probably one of the most important reasons to have good technique, so that you can be confident in what sounds will come out.

I Don't Know How to Warm Up My Voice – I Do What I Think Is a Warm-up and Still Crack Notes

Warming up means exactly what it says on the tin... It's starting to work the muscles so that they are warm and flexible and you aren't just singing on muscles which have been 'asleep' and therefore easy to injure.

Most people attack a warm-up with far too many huge riffs (a flashy series of notes) and loud singing. The best way to warm up is gently and gradually, and to combine your warm-up with a bit of technical practice.

I Know I'm a Good Singer. I Record Myself and Listen Back. I Can Sing So Much Better than Many People, but I Have No Confidence in Public

Controlling a wobbly, nervous voice as we spoke about above can be done with breathing technique. However, controlling your mind and stopping negative, unconfident and destructive thinking is something that a totally holistic view of vocal technique will help you with.

Unlike a piano player or a guitarist, your instrument is inside you, and if you are upset, then your instrument – your voice – won't work properly. However, be assured that you are not alone. Self-doubt is something that most singers feel at some point in their careers. It's not possible to avoid completely as we are all human, but it IS possible to know the many techniques to deal with this when it rears its ugly head. I will cover these throughout the book and particularly in Chapter Fifteen (page 173).

Everyone Says I'm Tone-deaf. I Think I'm Singing the Right Note but Everyone Says I'm Not!

If you are actually tone-deaf, I'm afraid being a singer maybe isn't for you. There are so many hurdles to overcome as a singer, and if you can't sing the correct notes then you will always have problems. In this case the best thing to do is go to a singing teacher for one lesson and establish whether they think your 'musical ear' is possible to train.

I Want Vibrato – How Do I Do It?

Natural vibrato (a rapid, slight variation in pitch) is present when the voice is produced properly. You will find that when your voice is in the right place and unnecessary tension has been eliminated, your vibrato will naturally appear.

I Have Big Breaks Between My Registers. How Do I Smooth Them Out?

Within a singer's range there are several registers. These registers are areas of different resonances and tones produced by a particularly vibratory pattern. All singers have breaks – it's just a case of disguising them, which can be done with specific exercises and understanding your own voice.

There are many more questions like these that will be answered throughout the chapters that follow. I intend this book to be an A–Z on everything you will need to know about being a singer, from opening your mouth in the first place to getting on the stage.

Happy reading!

CHAPTER SIX

EVERY BREATH YOU TAKE...

BREATHING AND SUPPORT EXPLAINED

When we singing teachers talk about breathing, the uninitiated perhaps think we are only talking about how long you can hold a note for and where to take a breath in a song. Of course such things are important and will be discussed later, but breathing is so much more than just that. Breath control and support are, in my opinion, the most important things you will ever learn about singing.

Support is the term we use to describe the appropriate type of breathing that can be used to totally control your voice and enable it to have the freedom to do whatever is needed. In all my years of teaching, even with many hundreds of people who have previously studied singing to quite a high level, only one or two people (yes, you heard me correctly: only one or two people out of hundreds!) are breathing correctly when they come into my studio. Some people have the right idea but not nearly enough muscle power, while others have it totally the wrong way round. Still more tell me they've had lots of singing lessons, yet very surprisingly, breathing doesn't seem to have been taught at all. Many teachers, apparently, have told them to 'breathe low'. Well, that's correct, but how on earth do you do it?

You may also ask, why do I think I know it all, as far as breathing is concerned? Well, it's not just me but many thousands of opera singers who have had to rely on their breath control and support to get them through incredibly taxing three-hour operas night after night. They must sing perfectly every show or the critics would be down on them like a ton of bricks – or worse still, they wouldn't be booked by any other opera houses. The pressure to perform the work exactly as the composer wrote it is immense, and the only way they can do this is by having a solid technique, the main basis of which is correct diaphragmatic breathing. In opera, it would be nigh-on impossible to even get through most of the roles without incredible support. Here, I want to pass on to you singers, many of whom will never have been to an opera (or wanted to go, for that matter), the secrets of singing with complete control. When you get it right, it feels so different and so right.

I must stress that you will not sound like a classical singer just because you breathe correctly. On the contrary, you will still sound like you, just better! Also, I'm not saying that every classical singer is perfect. There are some shockers out there, believe me – you might have heard some. What

I AM saying, though, is that diaphragmatic breathing is given much more emphasis in classical singing because it's virtually impossible to sing correctly without it.

Why then wouldn't we all want to learn to that level of perfectionism?

I'm also not saying that it's only opera singers who have great breath control, but most of them do breathe incredibly well. That's where I learnt the technique and I want to share it with you. So let's be as good as we can be. Read on and we'll find out how...

Perfect Posture

Without good posture, we cannot get the full benefits from our breath control. You may argue that when singing at a gig you might want to slouch over your guitar or slump over the piano, and not stand upright looking like a wally! Let's just say that once your technique is solid, you may be able to be a bit more easy-going with your posture, but I always tell my students that when you are learning, your posture needs to be perfect in order for that stance to become your 'neutral' – your automatic choice or your 'go-to place'.

And yes, while learning many of these things, you might feel like a wally at the start, but just remember, you are thinking like an ATHLETE and every athlete has had to practise the proper stance for their sport for hours on end.

Correct posture prevents unnecessary tension in places where it isn't needed. It would be wrong to say that we want a relaxed posture. When relaxed, we often slump our shoulders, and although we don't want raised shoulders, neither do we want them slumped.

Tension is a funny word, because without a bit of tension or resistance in the correct muscles, we wouldn't be able to sing. However, the wrong tension is no good to us. Athletes need to have tension in the muscles they use to perform, as do singers. We need athleticism and energy in the muscles, and in order to achieve this, a bit of what I will call 'necessary tension' is essential.

First, stand with your shoulders sloping down but not slumped. I always tell my students, 'Shoulders down, boobs out!' By that I mean a proud sort of stance, as if to say, 'Look at me!' Your arms should be by your sides but not rigidly held in place as if glued to the body – there needs to be a bit of space under the arms. Imagine you have perhaps a large orange or a balloon tucked under each arm. (Perhaps the balloon is better, because I don't want your arms to have to squeeze too much to keep it in place!)

Your feet should be hip-width apart (or slightly less depending on the width of your hips!) and your knees shouldn't be locked into place but a bit relaxed.

Your spine should be aligned, which means that each vertebra should stack up properly, none of them out of place from the one above or below.

You will hear many teachers go on at length about 'postural alignment', but all this really means is that you need to stand up with a nicely straight but not overly extended spine.

An exercise I do with my students is to stand against

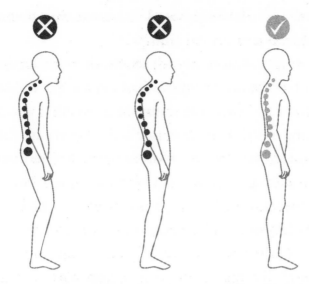

the wall with their knees bent. The idea is to press your back into the wall and feel every one of your vertebrae in the correct position, like sitting in an upright position on an imaginary chair. It's good to sing in this position for a while, and then when you stand up away from the wall, you're more aware of your spine.

I always get my students to stick their pelvis out.

Then stick their bum out.

Finally, I ask them to find a neutral position between the two.

When the pelvis is aligned properly and the spine is correctly set up, proper diaphragmatic breathing can take place. Also, with correct postural alignment, the airways can be kept open and the breath – and therefore the sound – can flow properly.

If your pelvis seems a bit 'stuck' when you sing, try to get hold of one of those big inflatable Swiss balls they use in the gym for stability, and rotate your hips and waist while sitting on it. You can even try singing while sitting on the ball.

Don't worry too much if you think your posture isn't perfect when you are singing. Just keep on checking in the mirror every now and then, and keep fixing it if it looks or feels wrong. Gradually, it won't be necessary to check it so much, and correct posture will be your new normal.

OK, assuming you now know how your posture ought to be – even if it's not quite perfect yet – you can go on to learning how to breathe using your diaphragm.

Diaphragmatic Breathing

People often ask me why they lose their voices after singing a couple of songs at karaoke, or they have no voice at all the next day after speaking above the music on a big night out. My husband, Gordon, goes to Arsenal matches and is hoarse for two days afterwards from shouting and singing football songs. (I'm sure other teams' songs make you just as hoarse but I wouldn't be allowed to mention them here – come on, you Gunners!)

As children, we scream and shout and sing loudly and don't seem to lose our voices as often as when we become adults (although children do sometimes get vocal problems too). Some of that is to do with changes in our bodies or larynx as we get older, but on the whole, the stresses and anxieties of adult modern life cause us to breathe in a shallow upper-body fashion, and we frequently 'keep hold' of our worries and concerns in our posture. This type of shallow breathing is known as 'clavicular breathing'.

People often turn to alternative therapies such as meditation or yoga to help them deal with stress. One of the first things these therapies will help you with is how to breathe more deeply. In singing, we also have to learn how to breathe deeply. For this we have to learn to breathe using our diaphragms. To learn to use our diaphragms to help us to sing, we must return to a totally natural approach.

If we saw something awful happening or someone in immediate danger, our primal or animal instincts would subconsciously kick in and we would pull our tummies in when we shouted. The 'fight or flight' mode would begin, and our subconscious minds would return to the natural way to scream, which is using our diaphragms.

Try it and you will see. Imagine you need to warn someone of a hazard, and see how as you shout, your waistband will quickly release and then contract as you scream or shout out the warning.

Here, let me explain the differences between clavicular and diaphragmatic breathing. If I say 'take a breath' to most untrained singers or anyone in the street, they would make a gasping noise and lift their shoulders. That is the shallow and sometimes tense and stressful breathing we use in our everyday lives. It is called clavicular breathing because the clavicles (or collarbones) are involved in the process.

As singers, we want to use diaphragmatic breathing to its best advantage, so read on and I will explain why that is.

The Diaphragm

According to *Collins English Dictionary*, 'The diaphragm is a dome-shaped muscular partition that separates the abdominal and thoracic cavities in mammals.' When it contracts, the volume of the thorax is increased and this inflates the lungs. It therefore plays a major role in breathing.

Here is my step-by-step guide to diaphragmatic breathing. The aim is to contract the diaphragm. When we do this, we allow more space for the lungs to fill up.

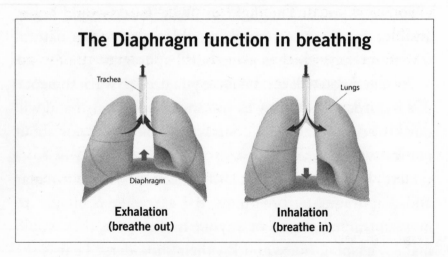

The Diaphragm function in breathing

Trachea

Lungs

Diaphragm

Exhalation
(breathe out)

Inhalation
(breathe in)

First, lie down on the floor with your spine flat and your knees bent. Now close your eyes and imagine that you are on a beach somewhere or wherever makes you feel relaxed. Place your hands on your tummy around your belly button.

Be aware of your hands rising as you breathe in and then falling as you breathe out. Get a gentle rhythm going and be aware of just how low you are breathing.

Now slowly get up. Put your hands on the same place on your tummy and feel the same movement.

We will now exercise the muscles that do this. First, check your posture (page 61) – your spine must be aligned for these exercises to work properly.

Exercise One

Pretend for the moment that I'm your personal trainer. At this stage I don't want you to think about 'breathing' – this is just a tummy exercise. We are doing this one just so you can allocate the muscles and get used to them being flexible.

Without slouching as you do this, let your tummy go 'fat' – this is quite a fast movement.

Now pull your tummy in quickly.

Do a series of ten of these: fat, in, fat, in, fat, in, etc. Think at this stage of pushing your tummy out; it will soon get used to it and it will be more of a natural movement.

Exercise Two

Again, this is just a tummy exercise but it resembles more of what you will eventually do when you are singing. After the first exercise it should be straightforward. This time you go 'fat' then you pull in for 'one, two, three, four' (just do the count in your head, not out loud). In other words, the 'fat' is just as fast, but the 'in' has four beats.

Again, don't think about breathing.

Exercise Three

In the first two exercises, we have made no sounds. Now we are going to combine a sound with what you're doing with your tummy.

Make the noise 'vvvvv' as in the beginning of the word 'voice'. The sound should resemble a vacuum cleaner. The idea is to hear the air, but more importantly to feel the tingle of the resistance of the 'vvvvv' on the lips. Don't conserve air: you want to use the full extent of your breath to make the constant 'vvvvv'. The more air you expel, the better 'fat' you will achieve.

And so this time the exercise is the same as Exercise Two, but making the 'vvvvv' noise during the 'in' stage of 'two, three, four'. Don't say the 'two, three, four' out loud, just make the 'vvvvv' noise for that length of time : 'fat, vvvvv, vvvvv, vvvvv'.

Do ten of these exercises if you can, but you may get dizzy as you will be breathing a bit more deeply than you normally do, so maybe start with five and build up to ten.

You are actually breathing 'properly' now, but I still don't want you to think about it. This way of breathing replaces your former loud, 'snatched' breath. Every place where previously you would have taken a breath, now just think 'fat'!

Exercise Four

In this exercise you will imitate a mobile phone on vibrate. Flexibility is key, so this exercise is one you can do at any time of day just to get used to how to make a sound while using your tummy muscles.

Make a 'zz zz zz' sound like a mobile phone vibrating, and use your tummy to make it. To do this, pull your tummy in to each 'zz' and immediately release it.

Now complete ten of these in a row – it should feel like a proper tummy workout.

Exercise Five

This exercise is about building up your breath control and seeing the results for yourself.

First, do a 'fat' followed by an immediate 'vvvvv' sound, but this time, instead of releasing your tummy, you want to keep pulling it in.

Imagine I'm standing behind you: I've hooked onto your tummy button from behind and I'm pulling it towards your spine very gradually.

Imagine it's an elastic rope I'm pulling with: I'm only going to let go when I've reached your spine. You want to keep going until you would keel over if you didn't stop, and every last bit of breath is used up. If you do that, then you won't have to think about releasing your tummy – it will release itself as your natural primal instinct to stay alive kicks in.

While doing this, time yourself to see how many seconds

you do. At this point, don't try to make a controlled sound. Usually, if beginners have a controlled sound, it is because they are using their jaw, chin or sheer tension for control. I would much rather you didn't cheat like that, and instead just let the sound come out wobbly, if necessary.

The average time when people's tummies release, when doing this for the first time, is around twelve seconds. If you get to twenty seconds, well done, but you can still work on building up your breath control. If you only get to seven seconds, don't worry, because you will quickly improve. It all depends on your shape, your general fitness level and how deeply you breathe naturally. There is no right or wrong number of seconds you can manage to get to as a beginner – what's important is that you improve.

Most of my students aim to beat me, but obviously, I do this every day so I'm hard to beat. Not many of them succeed, but here I must give a shout-out to Howard Lawrence from Disclosure, who after a few lessons sent me a very excited text to say he had done sixty seconds! Now that's impressive but also pretty extreme, although by all means challenge him to a breathing duel.

Exercise Six

Now, instead of one single note for your 'vvvvv', you can start singing up the scale. What that means is that you should pick a note in the middle of your voice, and for the sake of argument let's say it's a 'C' (don't worry if you don't understand musical notes, just find someone who does to sing a scale into your phone and copy that).

Now sing the sound 'vvvvv' on the following scale: This can be any note that feels easy for you to start on.

And so on.

Remember, as you sing, your tummy will be coming in, and when you stop singing, it will spring back out again. This technique is known as a 'recoil breath'.

As you are still learning to use these muscles, it won't yet be automatic, so encourage your tummy to move in and out; perhaps put your hand there to feel it happening. But don't be tempted to use your hand to push your tummy in: your tummy has to build up its own strength.

This will seem like hard work, but you will thank me when you have a six-pack!

Don't do too many scales at the moment – this exercise is all about controlling your breathing and not, at present, expanding your range. It's best to do around five perfect repetitions rather than fifteen bad ones. Generally, that's very good advice for most of your singing practice. Five minutes of intense concentrated work is much better than singing without technique for an hour and simply tiring yourself out. Just work for as long as you can keep focus and concentration, and then build this up.

Summary

Let's review what you have learnt in these exercises:

- In order to breathe deeply, we must use our diaphragm, which divides the lungs from the lower internal organs.
- We want our abdominal muscles, that is, the whole area above and below the belly button, to come out (or go 'fat', as I always say). As this happens, the diaphragm simultaneously contracts and goes from dome-shaped to flat. This action draws air into the lower lungs and causes the ribcage to open. To achieve maximum results, you should feel like your whole abdominal area, both high and low, front and back, is like a big fat barrel.
- Remember, although a lot of my exercises are concentrated on the tummy muscles, we need to expand all the way round, not just at the front – think of the barrel I just mentioned. You don't want to feel like your barrel is stuck in position, but you do need a certain resistance keeping the flow and posture as you breathe out, otherwise it would all just suddenly collapse.

This technique uses our abdominal muscles to help resist the sudden relaxation of the diaphragm, so we are keeping a support for the breath flow.

I always liken support to a very posh fountain. Imagine a fountain in Vegas that is controlled by computers. Every day the water flows evenly to exactly the same height, hour after hour. If we put a ping-pong ball on top of that fountain it would bounce very calmly at exactly the same height because the fountain is reliable.

Imagine a very cheap, pretty useless fountain – no computers, no set height, just a trickle or a whoosh depending on the water pressure. Put a ping-ping ball on top of that fountain and it wouldn't know what to do. One minute it would be flying up in the air, the next there would just be a tiny tremor.

Your voice is the ping-pong ball. If you give it regulated, consistent, reliable breath flow then it doesn't have to work hard, it knows it will be controlled and it won't fall off the fountain. However, if you give it sporadic, unreliable breath flow then it will be pushed one minute and not have enough oomph the next.

Of course in real life, we have to vary the amount of breath we give to certain phrases or notes, so it isn't as easy as controlling a computerised fountain, but you get my gist. The more consistent your breath support and flow, the better. From now on, instead of taking a breath that is an audible gasp, you will just go 'fat' instead. This general expansion all the way around your torso is your new 'taking a breath', and all this takes place in the lower part of your body while the top of your body remains relatively still.

I always say imagine you are a newsreader when practising your breathing. Above the news desk we would see nothing but calm, while below the desk your abdominal muscles and diaphragm would be working like crazy.

71

Now let the air come in through your nose rather than via a gasp from your mouth (however, please note that when you are actually singing a song, you will be breathing through your mouth).

Remember, proper breathing is relatively silent – the only time we should hear your breath is when you are using the sound for dramatic effect. Sometimes, for example, at the beginning of a pop ballad when we are trying to sound upset or passionate, a dramatic breath can be used. However, your new default setting is low silent breathing.

Think about it: if you want your voice to be Vegas standard, GET WORKING!

CHAPTER SEVEN

MY INFALLIBLE GUIDE TO WARMING UP

(AND WHY YOU OWE IT TO YOUR VOICE)

One of the things that singers who come to me for the first time often ask is how to do a warm-up. Even though they perform a lot and work hard on their voices, many of them don't have a regular warm-up that they do. If this is you, don't worry, you are not alone! In fact, I confess that even when I was studying singing at music college, I found it hard to warm up. I was fine when my teacher was there, but when I did them by myself, my warm-ups used to tire me out.

My first bit of advice about warming up is that different voices take different amounts of time to warm up; also, it all depends on how you are feeling on a certain day. If you are performing every day and your voice is regularly exercised, your warm-up may feel easy and not take long. If, however, you have been on holiday and haven't sung for a few days, your muscles might be lazy and it could take you a while to warm your voice up.

If you haven't had much sleep, or you were drinking the night before, your voice may not respond very well at all. And if you have had a cold and phlegm, it can take a long time to shift it.

When warming up, I always advise singers to do it in small bursts. Also, a great many people try to do too taxing a warm-up and tire themselves out. Successful warm-ups can be incredibly simple.

I'm not very good in the morning so it takes me a while to wake myself up, let alone my voice too. If you are like me, make sure you don't just get up half an hour before you are due to sing at a rehearsal! Get up a bit earlier if you have an important day of singing ahead, to give your voice a chance to wake up.

First, you need to rehydrate. It can take hours for the vocal folds to be rehydrated after a night's sleep, so start drinking water as soon as you wake up. As I said earlier, there's no harm in having your morning coffee if that's your usual breakfast drink, but remember that caffeine dehydrates you. If you do drink any caffeinated drinks, remember to drink a lot of water to compensate. Hot water and lemon is always a good alternative; perhaps add some ginger. A nice cup of hot water is always soothing. I find my morning hot drink is a bit like inhaling stream: it feels like it is opening my airways. A steamy hot shower has the same effect.

Once you have had some water and maybe a nice hot drink, start your initial warm-up by walking around the house, doing a bit of humming. Start on a note that is very easy for you – not too high – and then just hum up and down your range very gently. Don't go too high yet; this is just you waking up your voice.

If you find it hard to know how to hum up and down your range, just choose a very simple song and hum that. 'Baa Baa Black Sheep' is an ideal one because it has a series of descending scales and so it's good for warming your voice but not tiring it. Don't start too high; start in an easy place in your range.

Once you feel fully awake and you have hummed a bit, go to the place where you do your singing practice, ideally somewhere with a mirror so you can keep an eye on any unwanted tension.

Start by bending right over and touching your toes, and then very, very slowly come back up, feeling like you are letting each vertebra get back into position one at a time. As you become upright, think of opening your chest and keeping your shoulders down and back. You should now have the feeling that you are taller and more 'open' than you were before.

Gradually let your arms come away from your body; lead this with your hands. Now let them settle in a position slightly away from your body, as if you have a balloon under each armpit. You can now move your shoulders up and down a few times just to release any tension, and move your head sideways towards your right shoulder and then your left.

Stand with your legs slightly wider apart than your hips. Make sure you don't lock your knees but keep them 'soft'. Aligning your body properly is important because you will have a much freer sound, and it's something you should always try to do when you are warming up or practising so that it becomes normal for you to have good posture.

As I said earlier, I want it to be normal for you to have good posture at all times in your daily life so that this will gradually happen when you are performing as well. If you just think of good posture when you are singing and not at other times, it will be unnatural to you and could cause you more tension rather than less.

I get concerned when I see singers suddenly standing up straight when a teacher tells them to, when it obviously isn't natural for them. I would rather you just stay the way you are than be unnaturally stiff. However, if you do think about it every day when you practise, it will hopefully become second nature very soon.

Once good posture is normal for you, you won't have to think about it. Checking your posture each day when you do your warm-up just keeps you on track.

Once you feel that your body is open and your posture is correct, you can then begin warming up your voice. I quite often ask singers to start with a bit of a chewing action just to get all the muscles in the face and the mouth moving.

Over-exaggerate the chewing and look as ugly as you can in order to get the muscles awakened. Make sure it is up-and-down chewing, not side-to-side. Keep the molars in alignment – a side-to-side chewing movement can be harmful. As you are chewing, you can massage your face just in front of your ears where you feel the 'hinges' of the jaw.

Now do a lip trill (it's like blowing a raspberry). If you're having trouble doing it, relax your mouth a bit like you are fed up and it will be easier.

Next, let's wake up the tongue by doing a tongue trill. To achieve this, just go 'rrrrrrrrrrr'.

If you can't do that, relax and try again: think of the different sounds you would have made as a child when you had no inhibitions. Do the sound of a road drill, or a lion roaring... whatever works for you.

You should now do a few yawns just to relax your jaw and open the back of your throat.

Now you're ready for some scales. A scale is a series of notes either ascending in pitch or descending in pitch. If you are not used to doing them, it will seem odd at first, but the discipline of doing scales helps to exercise your voice and it also helps your musical ear to develop. You can do this unaccompanied as long as you know how the 'melody' of the scale goes.

If you have a keyboard and can play the scales before you sing them, this will help. Or just play the first chord of every scale.

If you are going for a singing lesson or have a friend who plays the piano, ask them to record the notes or the chords on the keyboard for you so you have something to practise with. It is much better to do this than to use a generic warm-up recording that may not be in your key. You can ask your singing teacher or friend to customise it for you and put it in keys that suit your range.

If you are using something that is commercially available or an app, that's fine, but don't keep singing if it gets too high or too low for you. Don't just switch it on and sing all of it without checking how you feel. Teachers stop and start during warm-ups to check you are doing it correctly and to adjust certain things. The danger with just pressing 'play' on a warm-up is that it's easy to strain if you don't pay attention and have no one listening to you. It's much better to do small bits of warm-up little and often until your voice feels warm than push yourself through a long warm-up, which tires you for the rest of the day.

Exercise One

Here is your first scale. Sing this on an 'ah' sound first of all. Check you have lifted your soft palate. To do this, put your finger onto the roof of your mouth behind your teeth – it will feel hard. Keep running your finger along until you come to a soft bit: that is your soft palate. The first thing I ask my students to do is to smell a rose. The set-up of this is to allow the singer to breathe through the nose and not the mouth, so that they can feel the continuous flow that comes from the lift of the soft palate and the depth of the diaphragmatic breathing. Here, we are talking about an absolutely gorgeous-smelling rose that makes us want to hold that smell and keep pulling it deeper into our nostrils. When you think of that, your cheekbones should rise.

You will be less likely to strain as you go higher if you have prepared by lifting your soft palate from the start.

I have written everything in the key of C for ease of reading but the idea is that you start these exercises in whatever key feels right for you and repeat them, getting higher or lower depending on the exercise and how your voice feels.

Exercise Two

Sing this same scale to 'ee' and then to 'oo'. Now put them together and get a lot faster. Start with 'ee' then 'oo' then 'aah'.

Exercise Three

Now we are going to do larger intervals (an interval is the distance between two notes). We will sing this to 'ee', 'ee', 'aah', 'aah', 'aah'. The 'ah' is on the highest note because it's an easier sound to open up with, but I want you to have your soft palate lifted and therefore the back of your throat open at the start of each exercise.

Get used to preparing for higher notes at the start of a phrase, because when we leave it too late, it makes it harder.

Exercise Four

Now let's check you are breathing! You are going to do the 'mobile phone on vibrate' exercise you learnt in Chapter Six (page 57). Remember, it's pulling your tummy in to the sound 'vvvv'. Refer back to that chapter to check you are doing this correctly.

Exercise Five

Now let's combine the third exercise with the fourth one. I want you to sing the notes of the 'ee', 'ee', 'aah', 'aah', 'aah' exercise to 'vvvv' or 'zzzz'. The idea is to think of the flow of your breath while singing. People often warm up and – I know this sounds crazy – they forget to breathe.

Exercise Six

Let's now open up a bit more. We will start the exercise by going up on a 'ng' sound, which should have a feeling of gliding upwards, then we will open out onto a 'yaah', 'aah', 'aah', 'aah', 'aah'.

The reason for the 'y' in front of the 'aah' is to give you a bit of energy for the second part of the exercise. Also, the 'y' actually makes you adopt an 'ee' position before you get to your 'aah'. An 'ee' gives you a sense of brightness and focus, which you want to carry through to your 'aah'.

I often find singing a 'yaah' energises the start of the phrase, and it's something you can incorporate into a lot of exercises.

Exercise Seven

Next, we need to be working the muscles required for articulation. This not only helps us to pronounce our words better, it also brings our sound into a good forward position that helps with resonance.

Pronounce the words 'red lorry, yellow lorry' very clearly and repeat. Sing these words on one note, over and over very slowly. Be aware of working the muscles in your face; not in an over-pronounced way where your face is moving about strangely, but rather in a way where you feel that it's the muscles inside that are doing the work.

Red Lo rry Ye llow Lo rry Red Lo rry Ye llow Lo rry

Red Lo rry Ye llow Lo rry Red Lo rry Ye llow Lo rry

Exercise Eight

Now for a downward scale to the words: 'unique New York, New York unique'. Start by singing those words on one note to get used to them, and then try going down the scale like this:

U - nique New York New York U-nique U nique New York New York U nique U

nique New York New York U nique U nique New York New York U nique

Exercise Nine

Now for a *legato* exercise (*legato* means 'smooth' in Italian):

'Yes you can sing'

Sing this exercise as beautifully and smoothly as you can.

Legato

Yes you can sing You can sing

Exercise Ten

Here is an exercise to give you energy: it's called 'the Yvie'. I used to do this with 'ee' but my students all used to end up adding a 'v' to it, so it has become: EE--Vee--EE--Vee --EE--Vee--EE.

Exercise Eleven

The following exercise is good for focusing our minds on the different ways we can start a sound.

'How are you? Are you happy?'

- We use an aspirate start (a sound with an exhalation of breath before it) for 'how';
- A glottal start (the vocal folds come together to close the glottis and airflow is obstructed. The glottis is defined as the opening between the vocal folds. Adduction occurs when the vocal folds come together to close the glottis) before the sound starts for 'are';
- A smooth start for 'you';
- And an aspirate start for 'happy'.

With the aspirate start, we will hear air prior to the start of the tone. With the glottal start, it is more of a stop/start onto the tone (if you can't find this sound, try in your natural speech to make the sound 'uh-oh' as if you were thinking 'Oh no!'). And in the smooth start, the breath and the coming together of the vocal folds happens at the same time.

As you do this exercise, be aware of the different ways to start notes. You should be able to do each of them.

How   are   you   are - you -   hap - py

Exercise Twelve: Falsetto

In order to exercise your falsetto, sing scales to the word 'who' – this encourages the airflow through the tone.

You should repeat this exercise up and down, up and down quickly in your falsetto range.

Who_____ Who_____ Who_____ Ooo

Exercise Thirteen

This exercise helps with forward placement and kick-starting your diaphragmatic breathing. Be aware of going 'fat' like we did when we worked on breathing (page 65).

As you start the exercise, which begins on a 'zzzz', simultaneously start the action of pulling your tummy in and then continue with this pulling-in throughout the exercise. But remember, you are not holding your breath; you are USING your breath.

Exercise Fourteen

When I studied 'bel canto', the word '*squillo*' was used often. It is a 'bel canto' term for a specific timbre that is brilliant, bright and very resonant, but it isn't just a sound that opera singers need. This bright, trumpet-like sound gives the voice lots of 'ping' and projection. It is therefore useful for all singers because it makes your voice a lot louder and edgier without any strain.

A good *squillo* exercise is 'mim', 'min', 'nee'. The sound should be bright and Italianate. You can do this exercise to a downward scale, like Exercise Eight, or to an arpeggio, like Exercise Three.

Exercise Fifteen

Once your voice is warm, you need to warm up your 'belt'. For this I usually use a shortened version of the melody of 'The Banana Boat Song'. A singing teacher of mine would use it years ago and it has always served me well. If you don't know this song, have a listen online. The belt position is employed in the first two 'day ohs' of each phrase.

There are hundreds of different vocal exercises you can do to warm up. The key is to start low and go high gradually. The reason for warming up is so that you do not damage the muscles by overworking them when they are cold, but also you will sound better if you have warmed up first. Warm-up exercises exercise your voice in the correct way, so you build up stamina and possibly range and volume depending on which exercises you do and how often you do them.

One final word of warning: never do an exercise if it hurts or feels wrong for your voice.

Check out my website for a link to these warm-up exercises.

Warm Down (or as I prefer to call it, 'cool down')

Like a runner or an athlete a 'warm down', or 'cool down' (as your muscles are already warm), is essential to allow the muscles to return to their neutral state. A marathon runner or sprinter will never finish a race and then just stop and sit down. First, they will slow the pace, and then walk and slowly relax the muscles with a 'cool down' routine of 'shaking out' any tension. They will also recover their breathing to a normal resting rate.

Equally, the vocal athlete (that is YOU!) will also work into their routine a cool-down process to allow the vocal muscles to release any unnecessary tension and to return to the neutral state so that the voice (ie. speech) is then relaxed and healthy.

The purpose of your cool down is to allow your vocal muscles to return to their normal speaking condition. This is particularly important when you have just done a big gig or a big day of singing. Perhaps you have noticed that at the end of a gig, your speaking voice feels very odd and tired. It is then so important to cool down with the exercises described below, to help your voice to get back to its neutral state so that any tension is released and your speech is free of huskiness or vocal fatigue. (And it's also important for singing teachers after a long day of teaching!)

Usually, I get my singers to first yawn to release tension in the larynx, and then from a comfortable speech position, pitch a humming descending scale of five notes (five, four, three, two, one). We then do some lip trills from the middle of the range downwards. Making a very low, creaky moaning sound, as you would if someone was massaging your shoulders and they got to just the right bit, is a good idea. It's also good just to move your shoulders up and down and let them collapse to a neutral position with a release of breath while making a sighing sound, which releases the upper body and brings the muscles back to their normal, neutral state.

Just think about yourself relaxing and letting any tension you have built up drift away with the release and flow of the natural level of breathing. That way, when you start singing the next day or the next session, you will hopefully be starting from a well-rested, well-relaxed place, free from any unnecessary tensions.

CHAPTER EIGHT

LET'S GET SINGING

It's hard to know where to start in this chapter, because obviously there's a lot to learn. However, as I've said before, my aim is to give you enough information to understand the basis of a good singing technique without scaring you off with too much. I will therefore start by explaining what to do and what not to do when trying to sing correctly.

First of all, let's think of your body as a whole. We talked about posture in order to get you breathing correctly earlier, so let's assume you are standing in your now-perfected, new stance. Imagine drawing a line between your lips and another line under your bust or chest.

Everything above line one has to work hard, everything below line two has to work hard, while everything in between doesn't do any work at all. This is of course

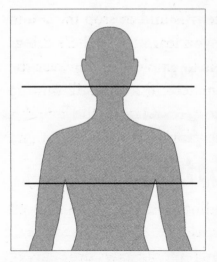

relatively speaking, and you know I don't mean it literally. However, what I want you to understand is that the muscles in the throat, jaw, neck and shoulders, which work overtime with untrained singers, are given a lot less work when the other parts of the body above line one and below line two get working.

On the BBC's *Strictly Come Dancing*, you often hear the judges talking about 'isolation'. What they are referring to is getting one set of muscles to work without the whole body having to move. It's the same with singing.

Sometimes we need to practise making sure that we aren't using unnecessary tension in the whole body to achieve a sound that is so much easier to make without that 'help', or rather, hindrance. For example, our tongues, our jaws and our shoulders often feel the need to participate when they are not wanted, so we need to be aware of when they are creeping in where they aren't welcome. Sometimes, some parts of the body or face want to compensate for a lack of technique. Certain muscles might work overtime because the muscles that are meant to do the job are not being used properly.

Let's talk about the jaw, for example. Before you were trained to breathe more efficiently, your jaw would have helped you to hold a note. When I watch untrained singers, I see the jaw stepping in to hold notes in place and control the voice, to articulate riffs and to stop the sound at the end of a phrase. When you learn to do these things with breath control, the jaw is unemployed; however the problem is that unless someone tells it, it will still turn up to work every day. So, let's work on relaxing the jaw; this will eradicate unnecessary tension and help the sound flow better.

Pretend you are about to fall asleep on the train. If you are actually on the train reading this, take a look at all the tired commuters who have dropped off. When we fall into a relaxed doze while sitting up, our jaws drop down. This relaxed jaw position is what you want for singing. I'm not talking about an overly extended jaw, just a relaxed one.

Try relaxing your jaw and saying 'blah, blah, blah' as if you are really bored by what I'm telling you. Massage your jaw a bit if it seems locked in a tense position. Now try singing a phrase in that overly relaxed 'blah, blah, blah' way. I don't care if it sounds flat at the moment. In fact, if it does sound a bit flat, you are probably doing it correctly.

Don't worry, I'm not teaching you how to sound flat! We are going to use other muscles to compensate for this. So let's assume you are now aware of a new relaxed position for your jaw. Use a mirror to make sure that it is no longer tense. It will feel alien at first but persevere.

We can now talk about the muscles that you will be using instead. Your jaw won't be controlling your sound, your diaphragmatic breathing will be. However, as we just discussed, no matter how well we're breathing, if we totally relax our jaws and do nothing with our faces, our voices can sound flat.

It's now time for the muscles above line one – for example, the tongue and soft palate – to be awakened, as explained in Chapter Seven (page 73).

That position of the cheekbones is vital for singing – it's what I call a 'singing smile'. You smile with your whole face above line one. Your eyebrows engage, your eyes sparkle and your cheekbones lift. Using these muscles gives your voice resonance, helps to keep it in tune and compensates for the newly relaxed jaw position you have adopted. However, it's a singing smile, not a normal smile: we are not grinning with our mouths; we have isolated the smile muscles to above line one.

We're not talking about holding the cheekbones in place in a tense way. With singing, there is always flow. Think of the smell of the rose flooding your senses or the music of your song flowing out of you. I will talk a lot about flow – it's a bit like golfers talking about following through when they've hit the ball.

Everything we do in singing is leading on to the next note or the next phrase, so there is a constant natural flow, which is often referred to as musicality. That's the difference between you as a singer and a football fan, for instance, who just sings one note after the other with no flow or link between the notes. Sorry to football fans who are fabulous singers! There must be a few...

Let's talk about your tongue. When I was first taught to sing, there was an understanding that a flat tongue was ideal for singing. Nowadays we know that a flat tongue can be a tense tongue, and tension in the tongue – especially at the root of the tongue – can impede our sound production. We want our tongue to be energised when necessary but not tense.

Let's go back to falling asleep on the train. When the tongue is relaxed, it isn't flat as we would have thought. It sits on the roof of the mouth, and the tip of it rests behind the bottom teeth.

Try making sounds with your tongue in that position. Now try the sound you make when you discover a cheeky secret, a bit of a downwards 'mmmm'. Then try singing a song. Your tongue will want to move a bit, but just try to be aware of it and don't let it go flat. Keep that tongue curve when singing.

Remember, all these exercises take time to get used to and to practise – don't feel you have to do them all at once and in one day. I often say to my students: I'm your personal trainer, you come to me in the morning, we work on all these muscles, and then you carry on your day without thinking of the muscles at all. Even at your gigs, just sing the way you have always sung and then gradually the two worlds will become one. It's much better to do it that way rather than try to do everything you have learnt at your first gig. An overload of information can put you off. It's much better to give yourself the time you need for your muscle memory to kick in.

A very useful tip which helps not only singers but anyone who uses their voice a lot, or who finds their voice gets hoarse or easily tired, is to exercise with straws. This exercise is also often used for singers who have damaged their voices, to help them get their vocal stamina back. The aim, according to Dr Ingo Titze, the eminent voice scientist who developed the exercise, is 'to stretch and unpress' your vocal folds.

Exercises like this, which use a 'semi-occluded vocal tract' (meaning the mouth is partially closed or the opening is narrow), maximise the amount of air pressure passing across the vocal folds. Similar practices include exercises on narrow vowels, sirening and lip trills, all of which I will explain later.

The straw exercise is very efficient because the pressure at the lips enables less muscular effort than open-mouth singing and therefore minimises vocal fatigue. However, it is important not to let air escape around the straw or through the nose. It is also important to feel that you are engaging the abdominal muscles as you are blowing on the straw. This is very much a breathing exercise which complements the diaphragmatic exercises we did in Chapter Six.

First, get some straws of different sizes – everything from large children's straws to small coffee stirrers. Start with the larger straws and progress to the smaller ones. Begin with the sound 'uh' and glide from a low note upwards then back down again like a siren.

Now make a sound like you are trying to rev up a motorbike. Use the shape of a siren as in the diagram below.

As I said before, use your abdominal muscles while making these sounds (see also page 69).

Now you can attempt phrases from a song through the straw. Take away the straw and try to sing the phrases using the same facial and abdominal muscles you have just used. Another way of saying this is that you are using the same 'set-up' – this 'set-up' helps your placement. Your straw exercise should have established a good placement for your voice. This is because you are using energy in the correct muscles. Every time you want to check your placement, go back to your straw and check what you did.

Now we are going to talk about vowels. You should always be singing on vowels to sustain vocal tone. If we can achieve perfect sounds on vowels, the consonants will look after themselves – or at least we can do articulation exercises to bring them in at a later date. Previously, I talked about 'bel canto'. Singing on vowels is the beginning of us working in that way.

Let's begin with an 'ee'. This is a bright, forward sound, which means it will be resonant and give your voice the necessary 'edge' it needs to project.

Now sing an 'ee' as in the word 'sweet'. Your mouth should be open but not stretched wide. Your tongue should be in the position we discussed earlier: arching slightly downwards behind your front teeth.

Our next sound is 'ay'. This is a happy, bright 'ay' as in the word 'day'. Don't think of the posh pronunciation of the word, which is too dark, but a more Italianate pronunciation, or even the way the Scots say the word. OK, I'm biased, but we do have nice bright vowels!

The only difference in the position of your mouth should be a slightly more relaxed jaw than with 'ee'.

We now have an 'ah'. An 'ah' is a very open sound, like the word 'are'. It should just come out freely and easily, without much effort. Your jaw further relaxes and you have a 'pleasant' but not overly excited look on your face.

For an 'aw' we don't need to change much at all from the 'ah' sound apart from your lips, which are further back for the 'ah' and now need to come forward to shape the 'aw'.

Finally, we have an 'oo'. This is like the sound you make with the exclamation 'Ooh!' It is brighter and more energetic than the spoken word 'who', for example – it's like we are excited about 'who' it is. Remember, it's more of an exclamation than a word, so give it a bit more energy. Everything is in a similar position to 'aw', except that your lips come forward.

Practise saying these vowels, then singing them slowly by themselves, and eventually putting them all together in a slow 'ee, ay, ah, aw, oo'.

Notice that there shouldn't be much of a dramatic change in your mouth shape apart from with 'oo'. The jaw should be relaxed at all times, and slightly more relaxed for 'ay' and 'ah'. The sound should feel free, and you should think about your diaphragmatic breathing while singing the vowels. Therefore, you are now doing two of the most important exercises at once.

Sing these on one note over and over a few times to perfect them, and if you want to, change to the next note above and do it all again. Do this every day and perhaps record yourself to see how pure your vowels sound and how controlled your sound is. The idea is that if you were coming to me for weekly lessons, all these things would gradually be added into the mix until you had an overall understanding of your voice, so don't feel that you have to complete everything in this chapter in one day. Perhaps go away and come back to the next bit tomorrow, or start again on your breathing and get to the next page when you are ready.

Fifteen minutes of proper practice is better than working for an hour in the wrong way.

Now let's talk about your soft palate. As I explained earlier, when singing, we should be lifting our soft palate. Sometimes it needs an extra bit of lifting to get a better sound. The only time you don't need to lift it is if you are aiming for a specific darker sound, but that should be something you choose to do, not the way you sing all the time.

As a singer, lifting your soft palate every time you sing should be second nature, but at the moment it might seem difficult. In order to practise the sensation of lifting it, think about suddenly getting a surprise birthday cake – think of that feeling of 'wow'. Does that make you aware of your soft palate?

Alternatively, think of the beginning of a yawn, or eating a potato straight from the roasting pan which is too hot, so your soft palate lifts up to avoid burning your mouth as you blow air over the hot potato resting on your tongue.

Whatever you think works best for you is fine. What you want is to be able to immediately lift the soft palate when you need that extra space.

OK, let's recap what you have learnt and let's put it all together. Up to now we haven't been thinking of songs, just sounds, but let's think of a song. Think of a beautiful slow song. For example, Take That's 'Rule the World', 'Lay Me Down' by Sam Smith or perhaps Whitney Houston's version of Dolly Parton's 'I Will Always Love You'. Think of the first line.

Now, before you sing it, let's do a technique checklist. At the moment this might seem like a big palaver without even singing a line, but eventually it will become second nature:

- First of all, get your posture right.
- Now be aware of your breathing.
- Check your jaw isn't ready to tense up.
- As you go 'fat' I want you to smell a rose and at the same time lift your soft palate.
- Now calmly and gently sing the first line of your song.
- Do this a few times or continue for a few more lines.

Eventually, having correct breathing, correct posture, a relaxed jaw and a lifted soft palate and cheekbones in place will seem natural, not alien.

Keep practising!

Now we need to talk about your larynx. The larynx is often called the voice box because it houses the vocal folds. The epiglottis (which is part of the larynx) stops food going into our lungs by closing when we swallow. When air travels across the vocal folds, they vibrate together and sound is made.

The larynx can move up and down freely. As a singer, it is important that you are aware of letting it feel flexible and not 'held'. The larynx wants to go up as we sing higher in our voices, but helping or encouraging it to sit freely in a lower position is beneficial.

You know that feeling when you have sung too much, your voice feels exhausted and it's difficult to go back to speaking? That is how too high a larynx feels. Swallow and yawn a few times to encourage it to settle back down. Think of making a low purring cat noise to release tension in the larynx.

If you are singing high notes, try to avoid reaching upwards. Instead, think of lifting your soft palate as we discussed above and try to be aware of your larynx in a buoyant low position.

For belting, the larynx will no longer be in the low position. I tell my singers to get into 'climbing a hill position' as Leona Lewis is in the image below. Belting is

© Getty Images

a highly emotional state of what is really sustained and supported 'yelling' or 'shouting', but it is without strain.

Put your hands gently around your neck like a necklace and feel your larynx in a low position. You also want a broadening or opening feeling in your neck to achieve optimum freedom from tension and a free sound, so as you put your hands around your neck, try to feel that too.

For the lower range of your voice, try to think of a neutral speech-like position of the larynx.

At the moment all these sensations in the larynx may seem strange to you, but as you get to know your own voice, you will know when it feels right and when that feeling of it being in the optimum place coincides with easy-to-hit notes.

Registers, breaks, chest voice, head voice, falsetto...

OK, what's it all about? Don't worry, many singers find all of the above confusing, and 'How do I deal with the breaks in my voice?' is probably one of the questions I'm asked the most.

Firstly, I never use the term 'break' myself; I prefer the Italian term *'passaggio'*. A 'bel canto' term, it literally means 'passageway'. And if you think about it, this is a much better way of thinking about those areas of our voice.

The word 'break' means something is broken; we wouldn't be able to get from one area to the other if, say, there was a break in the middle of the road. However, if there is a passageway (or *passaggio*), we can find a way through.

The *passaggio* is like a transitional area that takes us from one part of the voice to the next. By lightening, brightening and changing the resonance of the heavy chest voice when going up through the *passaggio*, and by giving the head voice darker overtones while coming down through the *passaggio*, you can learn to deal with this area of the voice very efficiently.

A well-produced voice with a solid technique can glide through the *passaggio* without the listener noticing a sudden gear change.

I tend to avoid the words 'head' voice and 'chest' voice because I feel it is better to talk about one complete voice, which of course will have different amounts of resonance in different parts but a consistency throughout. However at the moment, because we are talking about how to deal with these parts of your voice, I will be mentioning these dreaded words a lot!

Falsetto is a separate thing, and controlling when you go into falsetto can be worked on. By nature, the pop falsetto sound is always breathy and light, and cannot increase in volume unless you mix it with some other voice components.

If you are confusing your head voice and your falsetto voice, do downwards scales starting on falsetto and bringing in 'head' voice on the way down, and then try the reverse.

Pop singers often want that 'flip' sound when going into falsetto, but it's good to be able to choose when you do this rather than it just happening, like a shock.

You can steal a technique from opera singers to develop the range of your full voice and avoid going into falsetto so soon. Sing a scale, and when you get to the note where your falsetto appears, instead of allowing that, tilt your chin slightly downwards and pretend you are going to sound like an opera singer (not too over-the-top, just slightly!) or that you are going to burst into tears. These thoughts will take you into a different place in your voice, which in turn will enable you to go higher in your range but remain in full voice instead of falsetto. So, give it a try and keep practising.

Gliding up and down your whole range is a technique used to help negotiate the *passaggi* – that's the plural of *passaggio*! Stick to one vowel or sound and lightly negotiate your way. A cheeky 'mmmm' is good, or the 'ng' sound, which I had to use for my many years of opera training.

I tend to get students to first glide downwards, because it is easier to add on weight towards the bottom of the voice than to successfully lighten it enough on the way up.

Taking a heavy 'chest' voice upwards has caused many people many vocal problems. Always remember your voice is like a pyramid shape: it is brighter and less thick at the top and fat and heavy at the bottom. The base of the pyramid is far too broad to fit into the smaller, narrower top section.

It is important to note that your head position shouldn't change much while working from the bottom of your range to the top and vice versa. It is especially important that you don't lift your chin to 'reach' high notes or dramatically tilt down your chin to reach the bottom ones. The only time you are allowed to slightly lift your chin is to go into belt position.

So, let's talk a little about belting. Belting used to be thought of as damaging to the voice. We have now accepted that as long as it is done safely and properly, it can be used without damage.

In order to find your 'safe belt', imagine you are shouting out to a friend who is at a distance: you are not screaming or yelling, just loudly making them aware you are here. You will have naturally lifted your chin a little, and your breathing will be slightly shallower than what we have been discussing. As long as you stick to this set-up while belting and don't try to put extra weight on the voice or change position, your belt should be safe.

Maximising the brightness, ping, edge or *squillo* of your tone will help to avoid taking the unnecessary weight into the belt position as you 'climb the hill' (remember the photo of Leona).

What you don't want to do is to take your chest voice too high in your range. This will result in a flat sound and can cause voice damage or strain. When we go higher, we have to amend the sound accordingly. Aim to stick to this advice to achieve high belt notes, don't just stick up your chin and hope for the best.

Belting is something that you want to make sure you are doing correctly, so if you feel unsure, try to check with a voice teacher that you are doing it right.

Vibrato (a regular, pulsating change of pitch) is something that we tend to have or not have naturally in our voices. However, it can be controlled very well with diaphragmatic breathing. Opera singers tend to have a lot of natural vibrato, but it is usually controlled so it will be the same throughout their range.

Pop singers don't usually want to have much vibrato, and

if they have a natural vibrato, they want to be able to control it so that they can use it or take it away when needed. This again can only be done with diaphragmatic control.

Musical theatre singers often want vibrato to kick in at the end of big, long notes. Many producers in studios don't like dealing with vibrato and ask singers to take it away, but it can then be difficult for singers to emulate the recorded songs when they have to perform them live. Sometimes singers have to explain to producers that their voices have natural vibrato, it's not something they are adding.

Good diaphragmatic breathing can help with an annoying vibrato that isn't pleasant. Often, singers have a vibrato at the end of notes that they find hard to control. This is because they are often not supporting the voice right to the end of the phrase, or they are allowing too much breath to come out at the end. Through practice with the breath, they can learn to stop the airflow rather than push air out at the end of a phrase, and this usually helps to prevent these wobbly phrase endings.

Don't be scared of vibrato and try to hold it back through tension. Be proud of your natural voice, and until you learn to control it correctly with the diaphragm, just sing the way it comes out naturally.

If you have no vibrato and want some, just work on developing your voice naturally and letting it be as free as possible with the best support possible. Usually, when the voice becomes more developed, its range increases and so does its power, and often a lovely, natural vibrato is achievable.

Also, remember that position we used to get high notes,

where we mimicked an opera singer or felt like we were going to burst into tears, and tilted our chin slightly down (pages 101-102)? Try that position in order to practise singing with vibrato – that set-up often helps you to achieve a natural vibrato.

All these technical aspects of singing are very important, but what is vital is that you practise them until they become automatic, so that when performing a song, you don't have to think about how you are going to control your voice or reach a note.

As I mentioned before, think of your singing lessons or the practice you do yourself as personal training. You do it in the morning and then you get on with using all the muscles you have worked on without thinking about them. Gradually it will seem normal for you to live your life with the newfound physique your personal trainer has given you. In the same way, it will become natural to you to start singing correctly and safely.

When performing, your technique needs to be at its best but it also needs to be reliable, so that all you have to concentrate on is what your songs are about. We often hear judges on talent shows criticising contestants for failing to connect with the audience. Often, singers fail to connect and to sing the song with meaning because they are so nervous about what their voice is going to do. That's why I harp on about technique.

Solid technique gives you so much freedom and confidence because you know your voice will be reliable. Once you have that confident feeling of knowing you can trust your technique, you will never look back.

My proudest moment, when working on TV talent shows, is when I see the singers turning that corner. It's a different week for different singers, but I feel an incredible amount of motherly pride for them when I hear the judges say to them, 'Wow, that was your best performance yet!' or 'I didn't know you could do that!'

I was so excited when Stacey Solomon hit notes she had never been able to before (on Series Six of *The X Factor*) that I ran onto the stage at the commercial break and got whacked by the jib (the camera that's like a big crane stretching above the audience's heads). The cameras were still rolling so we have it on film somewhere; it's very funny. The only thing I hurt was my pride.

The other important aspect to gaining confidence and being able to totally concentrate on the meaning of your songs and your performance is learning your songs. But the art of learning deserves a whole chapter to itself (see Chapter Ten). It's obvious though, isn't it really? If you come on stage nervous that you might forget your words or which bit of the song you are singing, that confidence and connection will go straight out of the window because all you will be thinking of is trying to get to the end word perfect.

OK, let's sum up. What we have discussed in this chapter is the basis of singing technique. If you really practise your breathing, exercise your voice regularly and correctly use the muscles and techniques we have talked about here, you will build up stamina and may improve your range.

My main objective is to enable you to sing for longer

without damage to your voice. Vocal health must be the be-all and end-all. Without a healthy voice, a career is always in danger. OK, we hear about one or two multi-millionaires who can afford to take time off if they need to have a few months' rest, but for most working singers, if you don't work, you don't earn. It is therefore vital that you are as fastidious with the prevention of injury to your voice as a working athlete would be with his or her body.

This is really the tip of the iceberg as far as singing technique is concerned, and if you are committed to learning and understanding even more about the things we have discussed, we will talk about how to choose a singing teacher in Chapter Fourteen. Alternatively, keep practising all of the above until it is automatic, and please let me know how you are getting on.

CHAPTER NINE

CHOOSING THE PERFECT SONG

How on earth do you go about choosing a song to suit your voice? Sometimes, with certain voices, it's very easy. Some people have a tone that certain songs just really complement. For example, if you have a breathy, contemporary tone, you might suit an Ed Sheeran song or maybe something by Matthew Morrison. If you have a high voice, you might want to show off those high notes by choosing a Sam Smith song. People with a dark sound or those who are influenced by jazz might want to sing an Amy Winehouse number or try one of the classics by Ella Fitzgerald or Etta James.

It's difficult though, because if you try to be too clever and sing something unknown, the audition panel, or your audience, might not know it; therefore the reaction to you might not be so immediate. On the other hand, if you sing a classic, your version will inevitably be likened to the original. What's more, many other people will have covered this song, so the dilemma is that the auditioning panel or audience might either love hearing it again or be sick of the sound of it. The truth is, there isn't a right or a wrong. It all depends on the way you sing it, who happens to be listening on the day, and a good deal of luck.

Choosing songs for your gigs is easier, because once you have tried all your usual songs out, you can slip in a new one; if it doesn't work, at least you know for next time. Try singing along with the originals of songs or recording yourself and then listening back. Obviously a lot of the choosing of songs depends on your range – in other words, the notes you can hit. If you can't hit the notes comfortably, you will always feel concerned about those notes.

I've discussed with you before the fact that you can change songs into keys that suit you, but the problem is that often, if it's a song that is famous for its high notes or its drama, it will lose a lot of its energy if you make it too low and vice versa. A song known for its richness of tone will sound odd if you sing it too high – it might lose its sexiness or its gravitas.

Sometimes, choosing songs is a big learning curve, and we only realise that certain songs don't suit us once we have tried them out in performance. If you remain in doubt, a vocal coach or a rehearsal pianist can give you advice on what sounds good in your voice.

I coach a few singers who sound good whatever they sing, which can make it really hard for them to find their own identity. If you are lucky enough to suit lots of styles, then sing what moves you. Sing songs that get to you when you sing the words, or songs that make you feel confident.

My advice would be to practise your chosen songs until it almost feels like you wrote them. Get to the stage where you can't even really remember the original phrasing, because your version is the only one in your head.

I once had to sing at a very big event after not performing at that level for ages, and I spent months practising one song. It seemed ridiculous, because when I was performing regularly I wouldn't have had the luxury of devoting so much time to a single song. It was, however, the best thing I could have done. The confidence I gave myself from learning it so well was incredible. Previously, I had always been a nervous performer, and I realised that I had never learnt my songs to that extent before. From that minute on, I rehearsed, rehearsed, rehearsed. I had conquered my nerves after a lifetime of fear.

It was the result of a lot of things coming together – maturity, technical security, preparation and confidence – but somehow I had discovered the perfect combination. It really proved to me that you can never be too prepared.

We talk about singing songs 'into' our voices so that the muscles know what to expect. In performance, you do not want any surprises. Things can happen on the night that you aren't expecting, but you should be so secure in your song and the way that you are singing it that no matter what else happens, you won't be thrown.

I'm back to my Andy Murray comparison. Murray and his coach rehearse every possible angle that the ball could come from. They practise returning the ball, no matter how brilliantly or surprisingly the other player hits it. The result of this is that he is rarely surprised.

I believe that you should know your voice like Andy Murray knows his opponents. If your voice does something different or sounds different on a certain note, you should be able to deal with it without a thought. Preparation is the antidote to nerves, so have this mantra in your head: 'Listen up, nerves, I'm not going to give in to you – I've prepared so well that you can't get under my skin.'

Choosing songs is quite different if you are a songwriter, because you will want to sing covers that represent your writing style. That's a good idea because it's hard to make your mark in the business if you don't establish your own identity. However, I work with some songwriters who specifically cover songs that show a different side to their personality. I must say, that isn't a bad idea either. If all your songs tend to be depressing and emotional, it's sometimes nice for your audience to see that in real life, you can be upbeat or have a bit of attitude. Sometimes, the more outrageously different you can be, the better.

Choosing songs for auditions, as we discussed earlier, is totally different, because you should be able to avoid showing any flaws and concentrate on your best points. Unless, of course, you have been asked to sing a specific song – then there is nowhere to hide.

As a general rule of thumb, remember that when choosing songs to learn, don't run before you can walk. So don't pick Whitney Houston's 'I Will Always Love You' as the first song you work on. Believe me, there are easier ones to tackle!

CHOOSING THE PERFECT SONG

Often, I start students on something like 'Killing Me Softly' (made famous by Roberta Flack, and later the Fugees), or even just the beginning of a song if the end is too hard.

The more songs you try out, the easier it will be for you to make choices. For this reason, I always recommend open mic nights. The more you try out songs in front of people, the more feedback you'll get, and the more you will realise which songs fall apart when you are out there performing and which ones really work.

My last bit of advice is for you to read the words of your song, get right inside the story of it. If you can mean the words and relate to the sentiment of them, you will perform the song so much better than one you can't relate to.

OK, I know I sound like I'm repeating myself; sometimes with my singers (yes, even the very successful ones!) I have to remind them of the same thing over and over again. I myself go to see my friend and singing coach Graeme Lauren for a refresher lesson every now and then. Often he suggests something that I know really well, and I think, 'Duh, that's obvious, why didn't I remember that?' That's why you need another pair of ears just to remind you of all the hundreds of things you have learnt and then forgotten again.

Choosing songs is so personal, but be guided. Some people come into auditions singing a pile of old rubbish, and the three minutes, or however long the song lasts, seems like half an hour. I soon switch off, and I can't even really judge their voice properly because I'm a bit bored.

I do try, in that situation, to have the courage to tell them that I didn't rate the song choice, because if no one tells you, you won't know. Usually I would then ask them to sing something else as well.

Don't be offended if people don't like the songs you choose. Equally, don't be put off if you think a particular song really suits your voice and you are adamant it's your best song. In the end, it's just one person's opinion. Mind you, if you get the same opinion from a few people, don't be stubborn: DITCH IT!

There are people in the business known as A&R, which stands for Artists and Repertoire. They are responsible for signing artists to a record label and also choosing songs for their artists. It's a very important full-time job, which only goes to show how difficult it is to get song choices right.

Before you make it big and have an A&R doing the choosing, do as much research as you can and explore as many different types of song as possible. Pick a country song if you are a soul singer, or vice versa, and change it into your style.

Good luck with your song choices. It's so important and so hard too but it can be incredibly fulfilling when you get it right.

CHAPTER TEN

HOW TO LEARN A SONG

The things that I take for granted because I have been doing them for years are the same things that most people ask me about. Later on there is a whole chapter of this book that hopefully answers the most frequently asked questions (pages 233–246), but this question deserves a chapter all to itself.

How do you actually learn a song?

It never fails to amaze me how many people turn up at auditions getting notes or rhythms wrong in songs. There is a big difference between 'changing it up' and basically just getting it wrong. Of course, how you change up a song is totally up to you. You don't need to take my advice on that, but here are the basic guidelines of what is really expected and generally acceptable. We are talking here about covers of songs you have to learn for auditions or performances.

First and foremost, you need to learn the original song correctly. If you are going to change it up, that only works if you know the original melody and rhythm inside out. Otherwise you get a sort of mix between changed notes and wrong notes, and you wonder why it just doesn't work.

The basic rule is to establish the original melody in the first verse and chorus of the song; then in the second half of the song, you can do whatever you want. That way, listeners will think, 'Oh yes, I know that song. I like that song,' and then, 'Wow, that's clever! I like that version.' Otherwise, they will just think you have got it wrong.

This is the way that most divas have forever performed huge soul songs: start simply (not necessarily quietly, that depends on the song). It can be extremely sassy at the beginning, but the original melody should be established before mixing it up with changes and riffs. Sometimes a song starts with a big riff, and that's fine if that is how the song is written. Or, if you make up a big riff through choice at the beginning, just return to the melody after that. It is quite normal for backing vocals to sing the melody in the last chorus so that the lead singer can go crazy with riffs and showing off – this is not a new phenomenon.

I've worked to these guidelines with every singer I've worked with on TV talent shows, because they give the singer the greatest 'journeys' in their songs. But I can't take the credit – I didn't have the idea myself, I stole it from opera.

In opera, we have 'da capo' arias. A 'da capo' aria has three sections: you sing the first section as written, which leads into a contrasting second section, before going back to the first section and basically ripping it up! I had been so used to doing this for years in operas that it seemed natural to me to do the same thing with pop singers. Soul divas have also been doing it forever.

But let's discuss how we learn the first bit properly before we get ahead of ourselves and get onto the fancy stuff. The secret to a great journey in a song is making sure you start well. Many people are so excited to get onto the high showy stuff that they are a bit slapdash with the learning of the so-called easy sections.

First of all, listen to your song over and over again, especially the beginning. Take it a bit at a time. Don't just assume that if it's a song you have heard many times, you actually know it correctly. There are many songs that I think I know, but when I sit down to learn them, I realise I've been making up the words and singing wrong notes for years! Pay attention to the rhythms as well – wrong rhythms will just make the song sound messy.

If it's someone's favourite song, and you come into an audition or perform it on a talent show and start badly, you will get a black mark against you in the first thirty seconds of your performance. Listen carefully or have a rehearsal with a piano player or your singing teacher to check it's correct.

Only once you know the song perfectly can you start to 'change it up'. So, how do you do that? This is something you might find difficult if you have never done it before, but after a while it becomes a lot easier.

Don't try to be too clever – even just changing one note in a phrase can have a big effect. Imagine you have sung verse one very softly and emotionally, and then your first chorus is bigger, but not very powerful yet. In the first phrase of verse two, perhaps turn the melody around, maybe starting with a higher note; later on in the verse, you could stress a passionate word by putting it on a higher note or creating a riff with it.

Your use of dynamics (louds and softs) will also help to make your version of the song interesting. Maybe try singing the beginning in a breathy tone you have never used before, and then change to a more edgy tone as the song gets more passionate. It's all trial and error, but when it's right, you will know: it will feel exciting and fresh to you.

Words are so important. Read the lyrics out loud, maybe in the privacy of your own room, and act out the words of the song. If the song is about being heartbroken and you have never experienced this, think of something else that has made you sad and use those emotions to imagine how you might feel. We can only communicate a song really well if we actually mean the words.

When I talk about acting, I'm not talking about putting on a false character – I'm talking about actually pretending it's you who is the character in the song. My drama teacher, Patrick Libby, used to get us to imagine a few different emotions – for example, to encourage us to feel happy, he used to say, 'On the beach!' and we would quickly go there in our minds, transported to a happy, serene, unworried state. We would spend ages imagining our beach scene in great detail so we knew exactly how we felt, and then gradually it would take us less time to be able to feel like we were there. Eventually, Patrick, in the middle of a lesson, could suddenly shout 'On the beach!' and we could tap into that emotion pretty quickly.

In a performance, you have to be like that too. You might come on stage a nervous wreck, worrying about walking in your shoes or whether your microphone is playing up, even if you can remember which song you are singing next, but you must be able to very quickly tap into the emotions of your song as soon as you hear the introduction. That's why it's good to practise acting your song and feeling the emotions as often as you can, because there will be lots of distractions on the night and you want to be able to get 'On the beach!' very quickly.

I'll often be rehearsing for a very important gig with a singer, and they will be standing there with no expression on their face. I'll say, 'Can you mean it this time, please?' and I've heard the same answer from dozens of singers: 'Oh, you know me; I don't like performing it properly until the night.' This comes from embarrassment about performing in front of us all in the rehearsal room. The singer prefers to leave it until the audience is there, but believe me, if you can get over that and 'perform' the song as many times as you can, no matter how embarrassing, you will have the emotions much more readily on tap.

When it comes to my singers, I'm a battleaxe – I just make them get over their embarrassment, and often we end up with tears because they have felt it so deeply. As a result we have so much better a performance on the night.

Sorry, Joe McElderry, I have to mention you here!

Joe was a great singer from day one when he was on *The*

X Factor in 2009, but the judges wanted more emotion from him. One day I went on and on at Joe until I reduced him to tears by making him mean the words of a sad song. We had a really good cry together, and lo and behold, the judges were asking him where on earth that emotional performance had come from.

It seems cruel to make singers cry, but if it wasn't for Patrick Libby, I wouldn't treat my singers like Oscar-winning actors! They thank me for it in the end. If any of you are nominated for an Oscar, please can I be your plus one?

The next question people ask me about learning songs is how to learn the lyrics. For me, the easiest way is to think of the song as a story. If you start at the beginning of the story and remember what happens in it, this will be a great aid to remembering the order of the verses.

For remembering choruses, think of different meanings or emotions in the chorus. For example, in the first chorus you are just stating a fact. In the second chorus you are beginning to get passionate about it, and by the third you are properly 'on one'. By now you are absolutely enraged or full of passion, or just determined to get your point across.

Of course, you might want to do some songs differently. By the end, you may have resigned yourself to whatever it is and be really calm and thoughtful. Naturally, this all depends on the arrangement of the song. If you are making your own track or you have a band or a pianist playing for you, you can go quiet and slow wherever you want, but obviously if you have a huge track under you then you will need to keep your vocals loud. Just play around really and do what makes sense for the lyrics.

Another fail-safe method for song learning is to write the words down, memorise them and then write them down again. Somehow the action of putting pen to paper makes the words stick in your head more easily. However, don't get too panicked about remembering words. We all forget them every now and again, even in songs we have performed many times.

If it is a serious problem for you, I have known singers who have gone for hypnotherapy to calm down because sometimes the worry can get out of control. Just remember, if you are singing and performing well, the audience often won't even notice if you make up a couple of words. The secret is not to let your face give it away. I often see performances (especially on TV talent shows) during which I wouldn't have noticed a wrong word or note if the singer hadn't grimaced and therefore let us all know.

The same goes for cracking notes or singing a wrong note or phrase. Don't bring it to our attention; style it out and we may not notice. Things that seem major to you quite often aren't major to your audience: most people aren't looking for mistakes; they have come to have a good time.

Of course, there are some really difficult songs out there, and many of you will have trouble singing some of the phrases. In most cases, the more you practise, the easier it gets. This is because our muscles memorise the melodies, so they 'know' what bits are coming up next. Once muscle memory kicks in, the song becomes much easier to sing. However, if there are still some notes causing you problems, take the phrase apart. Sing it on your easiest vowel rather than the words, because maybe the way you are saying the words is hindering you.

If that feels a lot easier, try noticing what you are doing differently when you are singing on that vowel. Is your throat more open or is your face doing more work? Is the vowel brighter than the word, and so on? Once you have worked out what is different, try to keep those things happening while you put the words back in.

If it doesn't work, stick to singing on the vowel for a few days; eventually it might become automatic to do it properly. The muscle memory of the correct way will kick in.

If the vowel exercise doesn't work, try singing on the sound 'ng'. Some of my first opera teachers used to make me do numerous exercises on 'ng' or 'oo'. Keep singing on this sound until it feels right and only go back to the words when you are ready.

If it's a certain note that you are finding difficult – quite often it's not even the highest one in the song, but you just can't work out why you are having a problem with it – first try the vowels and the 'ng', and then if that doesn't work, try looking at the note before the difficult one.

I find in many cases with my students that when a high note is coming up, they tense up on the note before it. Sometimes they make the note before it very dark (I'm talking about a heavy vowel sound). If that happens, try thinking of a nice bright sound on the note before the difficult one. In many cases this will solve your problem.

The reason for this is that we have to think of the voice

like the gears of a car. If we want to get to fifth gear (that's the high note), it's going to be difficult if we are going straight from first gear (the dark heavy vowel sound). It's much easier if we get into third gear on the note before the high one (a nice bright vowel sound), so that we are ready just to pop from third to fifth, which is so much easier than first to fifth.

All these tricks of the trade are things that you can make use of over and over again in different situations. The more you get to know your own voice and your own bad habits or the things you struggle with, the more you learn how to fix them.

It's a great feeling while practising if you solve a problem yourself and learn how to sing that song a bit better. The old saying 'practice makes perfect' is certainly true when it comes to singing. As long as you are practising in the correct way and not straining, your voice will get stronger and easier to control the more you practise.

You know of course what I'm going to say now. Yes, my overused analogy: you are an ATHLETE, and we aren't training for a 5K, we're aiming for a FULL MARATHON.

On your marks...

CHAPTER ELEVEN

HOW TO PREPARE FOR AN AUDITION

The *Oxford English Dictionary* defines an audition as: 'an interview for a role or job as a singer, actor, dancer or musician, consisting of a practical demonstration of the candidate's suitability and skill'. In other words, it's not like a normal job interview where the interviewer takes on trust that the person in front of them can do all the things they say they can do (based usually on references). In a singing audition, you have to prove it.

It's a bit unfair really, because a maths teacher doesn't usually have to do sums at an interview and a cleaner doesn't have to show how well they can polish. But a singer has to actually demonstrate just how good they are on that first meeting. And there's no doubt about it: learning how to audition is just as important as learning how to sing. There's no point in being amazing at what you do if your legs turn to jelly as soon as you turn up at your audition; you will fall at the first hurdle.

As with most things in life, we do a much better job if we prepare. When baking, for example, if you're lazy and just shove all your ingredients into a bowl without measuring and weighing them out in advance, you may, with one out of ten cakes, be lucky and achieve a delicious result. But it's much more likely that you'll end up with a disappointing mess. In the same way, if you don't prepare for your audition, you may be lucky and sing well, but it's a high-risk policy. Much better to know exactly what you intend to do so that there are no surprises on the day – for yourself, as well as for the panel.

So how do you prepare?

Song Choice Is Vital

I often sit on panels, and I'm constantly surprised by singers saying they can't decide what to sing. They hand me a big list of ideas. But it's not up to ME to choose! I don't know what suits a particular voice, especially one I've never heard before. So be decisive, make your choice, and then concentrate on preparing that one song, making it as perfect as you possibly can.

What you should be absolutely sure of is your own ability, and whether you want to show off your voice in a really easy song or if you're willing to take a risk. And you're the only person who knows that.

I like surprises. Someone might walk in with a boring song but sing it really well – that's what's going to make me sit up and take notice. On the other hand, if you choose to sing something slightly taxing, it may show a few flaws but it will also demonstrate passion – and we all like that.

Don't put in a series of riffs just for the sake of it, though, because you'll detract from the true emotion of the song. I want to see and hear you meaning the words. If you're too busy thinking of your riffs, it will take away from that.

People often ask me whether they should accompany themselves on guitar. I can't say you should never do that, because some panellists really like it, but for me personally – and I speak as a singing teacher – I don't much care for watching people slumped over their guitars, concentrating on getting their chords right and making little or no eye contact. I always think they'd have come across more effectively if they'd just stood there and sung.

Having said that, if you're a guitar-based singer-songwriter, then go for it! I love people who know their own strengths.

How Do You Choose?

I'm not saying it's easy, but many people make choices for the wrong reasons. A common mistake is to pick a song simply because it's in the charts. But just because it's current and everybody knows it, that doesn't make it easy to sing or make it the best song to showcase your voice.

For example, when Adele's 'Someone like You' was first released in 2011, every other person, it seemed, sang it at auditions. But unless you have Adele's passion and ability to make us cry, it can be a really dull song choice.

It can also quite quickly demonstrate your inadequacies in comparison to the woman who co-wrote the song and made it a global hit. If you do choose that song, you should be aware that a hundred other people will be singing it too, and therefore you need to do something very different with it to make your version stand out. Much better to choose another less well-known Adele song, if she's someone you admire, which will give the panel a little bit more variety.

But for every hard and fast rule, there's an exception. I always say that I never again want to hear someone's version of John Legend's 'All of You' – then an auditionee will walk through that door, sing that song and absolutely blow my socks off. So don't be afraid to challenge me if you really feel strongly that an exceptionally famous song is your best option. Even so, in my experience, there are other songs that should be avoided at all costs unless you can bring something truly unique to them. These include:

'At Last' by Etta James
'Summertime' by George Gershwin
'Somewhere Over the Rainbow' – the Eva Cassidy version

If any of these songs is your true favourite and you're sure it will get you through the first audition, then by all means choose it, but if you can, try to change it up a bit. Listen to old auditions or YouTube or Live Lounge versions of songs to get ideas of what works when playing around with something.

As well as these song choices being predictable because

they're chosen by too many people, another reason not to sing particular songs is because they're too easy and don't challenge you or show off your voice.

Many auditions will be 'a cappella' (unaccompanied), so you need to be absolutely certain your song really sounds good without a backing track. Many chart hits have strong backing tracks, which are part of the reason why the songs are so successful. Take away the track and the big production, and the song itself can be dull. Also, songs by singer-songwriters that are laid-back and create a particular mood or feeling may be great when they're sung by the original artist in their quirky, individual way. But when sung by you, in a bare audition room, with no guitar and no track, it might just be awkward. Songs with very little range often become hits because of the words or the tone of the singer's voice. Again, their weaknesses may be exposed if sung by your solo, unaccompanied voice. And unless you have a better tone than the original singer, which is unlikely, or you have an amazing way of portraying the words with no accompaniment, it could all fall a bit flat.

A good example of a song which shows no range without a backing track and doesn't work without the original artist is 'The A Team' by Ed Sheeran. I have nothing against this song but it doesn't have high notes or difficult parts and doesn't ever seem to show off anyone's voice when I hear them singing it.

Another type of song that you should avoid is the diva-style, too-difficult-for-most-people selection. Everyone knows that Whitney Houston, Mariah Carey and Freddie Mercury are or were all incredible singers. And if you're as good as any of them, I can't wait to hear you! However, most of you reading this may not be quite there yet. So hold off on any of their songs, which you'll probably only get halfway through before you start straining your voice and cracking your notes. However, if you really want to sing them, these artists all have some easier songs, so pick and choose from their wider songbook, making sure to steer clear of singing anything that would draw attention to your shortcomings. I would go for one of their upbeat songs, such as Whitney Houston's 'I Wanna Dance with Somebody' or Queen's 'Crazy Little Thing Called Love'.

Which Songs Really Work?

Any songs work, even the ones I've told you to avoid, if you have an outstanding way of putting across the words and emotions and you have the most incredible tone. But few people have all those things, so you must decide what your strengths are and how best to show them off.

What Are My Strengths?

Here is a list of strengths a singer can have. Which of these fit you?
1. Great range, lots of strong high notes.
2. Quirky sound, really unusual stand-out tone.
3. Musically gifted, plays instruments, writes songs and has a feel for any song they sing.
4. Good in unusual genres – for example, classical, country, rock.

5. Moves people to tears when they sing (for a good reason!).

If you have any of these qualities, make sure you show off these individual strengths when you audition. I've had classical singers who've come in and sung a wobbly version of Katy Perry, and when I've talked to them afterwards, they've said: 'I didn't think you'd want classical.'

Sing whatever shows your voice off best. If you're a classical singer, you may be brilliant at that, but rubbish when it comes to Katy Perry. It doesn't matter what you think the auditioning panel might want. Always sing what you're best at, and that way, we'll sit up and take notice. If you sing something you imagine we'd like and sing it badly, you won't have another chance to sing another song and we'll never get to hear you at your best. Of course, if you're auditioning for a specific part in a musical, you have to sing what you've been asked to prepare. That makes life easy as the decision is out of your hands.

A word of warning: whatever you do, don't sing your own song at an audition. We won't know it, we've never heard it before and we'll be concentrating on that and not on your singing. Always sing something we'll recognise; this gives you a much better chance.

Naturally, most of us also have genuine weaknesses that we don't want to highlight in an audition. That's understandable. You don't want, for example, to sing a really high song if you haven't got the notes (or you sound a bit strained up there), or sing a very exposed soft song if your voice wobbles a lot.

Sometimes it's a bit obvious to a panel that you have gone for an easy option and we might ask for another song as well, but it's good to be clever and hide any flaws. Don't worry – we all do that.

Just make sure that you emphasise the things you are good at, whether that be connecting with the audience or singing with a fabulous tone (or whatever your thing is)! That way we perhaps won't notice any weaknesses you aren't keen for us to hear.

All right, so now you've chosen your song and you know how good your friends, family and singing teacher think you are. How else should you prepare?

Learn Your Song Properly

I know this may seem like common sense, but in that case, why do I hear hundreds of examples of people singing the wrong notes or the wrong words, or stumbling through the song and stopping in the middle? Is it just nerves, or is it perhaps that they didn't learn the song properly in the first place? Read on!

HOW TO LEARN A SONG

The first thing I recommend is to try and understand the meaning of the song. It's so much easier to learn the words if you think of them as a story. If you remember them as little more than a string of words, it's easy to lose your place when nerves kick in. But if you're telling the panel a story, it's much less likely that you'll lose your way in the middle. It's also so much easier to move the panel or make them warm to you if they genuinely believe what you're telling them.

Apply the story of the song to yourself. If you're fifteen and have never been in love or had your heart broken and find it hard to relate to that story, then make it about a friendship or your dog or your grandma. Whatever makes you put across the words with conviction – even if it's not what the songwriter intended – will make your performance better than if you're just singing words and not meaning them.

I can't count the number of times I've heard people singing beautiful love songs to me as if they were singing about their shopping list or what they had for their tea last night.

Singing isn't just about hitting notes and sounding good, it's about making sense of the words you're singing, otherwise you might just as well sing 'LA LA LA'.

Once you've learnt the words, make sure you know the notes and rhythm. Listen to the original artist and check you're singing it exactly like them. Yes, I know I said it's good to change up a song, but ONLY when you know the song properly and have learnt the original.

Changing up usually means changing a few things in the second half of the song. Be extra careful not to hit any wrong notes in the first half, or the whole thing will sound like a mess.

Breathing

I've covered breathing, warming up and a few vocal exercises in much more detail elsewhere in the book, but when you learn a song, you need to plan when to take your breaths and stick to that. If you haven't planned and practised where to breathe, often you end up taking breaths in the middles of words, which is never a good idea. (OK, I can think of an example where an amazing artist has done just that – R. Kelly in 'I Believe I Can Fly' – but on the whole it's to be avoided.)

Learn from Experience

If you talk to a lot of stars who took a long time to make it, they'll invariably tell you that they learnt from their mistakes. So my advice would be to try and do as many auditions as you can, even if it's for something you're not sure would be right for you. Or go and do open mic nights.

If you're a musical theatre or operatic singer, maybe go and get some experience at a local amateur dramatic club to see if you're up to the standard of the other singers. Whatever type of singer you are, the more you perform and the more opinions you get, the more you'll understand yourself as a singer and the more you can develop your talent.

Practice makes perfect, and there's no substitute for the real thing. You can't audition in your bedroom; you have to be in front of an audience, no matter how big or small it may be. It's really important to get a reaction. If everyone always goes crazy for a particular song – never mind whether you like it or not – listen to what you're being told. You can't hear what other people can hear, so you may not be the best judge of your ability.

Testing yourself on an audience is best. But it's also useful to record yourself on your phone and then listen back afterwards. It's not foolproof but it will give you a fair idea of how you sound.

It's fine to sing to your family just for practice, but don't always listen to them because they're probably a bit biased. How many times have you watched friends and family off stage screaming for little Johnny on a TV talent show and saying how brilliant he is? And how many times has the viewing public at home known that little Johnny's mum, dad, auntie and uncle are all deluded?

This is a personal opinion, but for me, the most important things in an audition are:

1. The emotion and the words;
2. Then comes the tuning and the technique;
3. Finally, it's the difficulty of the song.

To put it another way: in terms of my reaction, I want you to affect my heart more than my ear.

When Nerves Kick In

However many times you may have sung a song, it's always possible that you'll 'dry' when it comes to an audition. And that's a simple case of nerves getting the better of you. So how do you guard against that happening?

As I've said, the best way to learn a song is through story-telling. But that can be quite difficult with a song that's repetitive. It's easy to lose concentration for a moment and think you're at the second chorus rather than the first, and then you're in trouble. There's not a singer in the land who hasn't experienced that. And it's scary – bad if you're singing at a gig, much worse if you're performing live on television.

Recovery is the key. Don't stop and apologise and offer to start again. Carry on regardless, even if it means repeating a verse you've already sung. You can always make a joke of it afterwards. Having said that, I remember an occasion when a singer early in her career was performing at a very important event and she lost her way. She stopped, explained what had happened and started again, and everyone afterwards said how brave and down-to-earth they thought she'd been. In the end, I guess it's not so much about how you've gone wrong but how you recover when you do. Whichever way you look at it, the main thing is to be able to get back on the horse.

If you're not sure of the words, write them down on a piece of paper. That way, you're much more likely to be able to memorise them. I always think it's a bit like writing them on the inside of your brain. It's almost as though you're constructing a map of the song.

In Summary...

- You know how good you are;
- You know the words;
- You know the notes;
- You know where you should be breathing.

Now it's time to take a good long look in the mirror and see what the auditioning panel will see.

CHAPTER TWELVE

ME AND MY AUDITION

(AND WHAT HAPPENED WHEN THESE FAMOUS FACES FIRST STARTED OUT)

No one is immune from the blind terror of the auditioning process – and that includes artists who went on to become household names. Here, a clutch of famous faces share their personal experiences and offer a few tips on how to leave a (good!) lasting impression.

Susan Boyle – *Britain's Got Talent* runner-up in 2009

'My advice for anyone doing an audition is to do your homework. Make sure you have learnt your song inside out and have learnt the words very carefully. Try not to be too nervous and don't be afraid of the panel, they are probably very nice. Just try to enjoy it.

'I didn't realise how well my *Britain's Got Talent*

audition had gone until I got that fantastic reaction from the crowd. I was just enjoying myself.

'I loved singing in front of Simon [Cowell] and the other judges. I had a wee crush on Piers [Morgan] so that helped a bit. It was such a great experience; I'd recommend it to anyone.'

Alexandra Burke – *The X Factor* winner in 2008

'My first ever audition was in 2001 for the TV series *Star for a Night*, hosted by Jane McDonald. I was only twelve. I sang "You Might Need Somebody", the Randy Crawford song. My mum [Melissa Bell, former lead singer of Soul II Soul] was the person who'd put me up for the show. She was the one who always encouraged me, my biggest inspiration.

'I was incredibly nervous. My knees were shaking, my palms were sweaty and that still happens to this day. I'm twenty-nine now and I'm always nervous before every performance, but that's not such a bad thing. I think it means I'm taking it seriously.

'I first auditioned for *X Factor* when I was sixteen, and got told I was too young for the show. I tried again aged nineteen and that's when I won. The fact I'd been rejected three years earlier made it even more nerve-wracking. It was the single most terrifying thing I'd ever done. I didn't want to have the door slammed in my face again.

'Luckily, I had Cheryl [Cole] as my mentor; it was her

first year of being a judge. She'd been part of Girls Aloud, a girl band that had enjoyed major success and that had been put together from appearing individually on *Popstars: The Rivals*. So she knew what I was going through and what advice to give me.

'What the whole experience taught me was that you should always be yourself in an audition. And there's no substitute for preparation: prepare, prepare, prepare. Yes, you'll be nervous, but don't let that overpower what you've prepared. My background had been singing in pubs and clubs, at bar mitzvahs, weddings and funerals. So if I was in an audition or singing live on TV, I'd close my eyes and picture myself performing somewhere I was comfortable – singing in a pub, for instance, or in my bedroom in front of my teddy bears. That's how I got through every single week on *The X Factor*.

'And I'm here to tell you, I've always found it the most frightening singing to an intimate audience – and that, of course, can be a judging panel of four people. But I make a point of listening to any constructive criticism because you should never think you've got nothing left to learn.

'On stage, though, I become someone different. I call that version of me "The Beast"; she's my alter ego and she helps me get through it all. The rest of the time, though, I'm just little old Alex from north London, hoping to make my family proud.'

Peter Dickson – leading voiceover artist and voice of *The X Factor*

'The singing voice is actually not much different from the spoken voice in terms of the mental processes and physiology. It's the specific techniques relevant to each that separates them. I could empty a room with my singing voice yet frequently fill rooms with my spoken voice. This is a curious thing and something I find endlessly fascinating.

'It all boils down to specific practice and training in your chosen discipline, but because singing and speaking share so many common attributes, I happen to believe that voice actors should take singing lessons and singers should take voice acting lessons. Why? Because the techniques taught by all good singing teachers – diaphragmatic breathing, breath support, articulation, head voice, chest voice, pitch control and so on – are all essential skills required by serious professional voice actors.

'Conversely, the skills we teach at gravyforthebrain.com, the world's largest online voiceover training company, are supremely relevant and valuable to singers. At the core of our teaching is the concept of "emotional connection" to what's in front of them. We've all listened to singers who are evidently not connected emotionally to the song. All the notes are pitch perfect and all the words are in the right order, yet something is missing. It's the emotional connection that can bring a feeling of truth and authenticity to a performance and turn it from an ordinary delivery into a spectacular one.

'So to achieve this, it's important as a performer that you understand your purpose, identify and visualise your audience (even if it's only of one), feel the emotional connection to the words and, crucially, acknowledge their impact on you the performer and allow that acknowledgement to further enrich your performance and to imbue it with truth and authenticity.'

Ben Forster – *Superstar* winner in 2012

'I was in a TV advert when I was ten and I sang in school productions – I was Danny in *Grease*, for instance. But it wasn't until I won a scholarship to Italia Conti that I really started learning my trade. My first West End role was in a musical called *La Cava* and then I was in a Beatles show called *All You Need Is Love*.

'Auditioning for both was terrifying, and it's no less scary today even though I starred in *Elf* and I've been playing the title role in *The Phantom of the Opera* for twenty months. Winning *Superstar* changed my career. Despite the fact I'd been in *Thriller Live* for two years, there I was queuing in the rain with what felt like five thousand people waiting to audition. I was thirty-one by then but it felt like going back to the beginning.

'At last, my turn came and I sang "Who Wants to Live Forever" by Queen. I was then put through to the next bit of the process. When it came to it, of course, I was taking part in a live TV show, something of which I had no experience. I'd be sitting in my dressing room, watching it on the monitor, and then there'd be a knock on my door. I'd walk downstairs and jump into the TV and start singing. It was bizarre. It never got any easier because you could always mess up in front of millions of people. There was never a moment when I didn't feel the pressure.

'I'll never not be nervous in an audition, but I have found that one way of partially controlling them is by smiling at the people you're going to be singing for. It's physically impossible to smile and be terrified at the same time.'

Mel Giedroyc – comedian, presenter on *Let It Shine* and former presenter of *The Great British Bake Off*

'There was one occasion when I'd been asked to come and audition for the stage show *Mamma Mia!* When I walked into the room, I was asked for my music. It took me a moment to realise they meant sheet music for the pianist to play. I hadn't thought to bring any, so I lifted my rather large 'boombox' on to the table and proceeded to sing a rousing version of "Children of the Revolution" by Marc Bolan.

'Needless to say, I wasn't really showing myself off to my best advantage for a role in *Mamma Mia!* and the phone call never came. The moral of this tale, of course, is that everyone has audition days which they can look back on with a laugh. But don't worry; there will always be another one around the corner.'

Aled Jones – singer, presenter and actor

'I'm the worst person when it comes to auditioning. I have the ability to convince myself that I'm not going to get the job before I even walk into the audition. And I hate being in a room with lots of other people who are all after the same job, I can't stand it.

'I have so many songs and monologues in my repertoire. But I only ever come out of myself if I get into conversation with the director and we discuss what else I could sing or perform. I just don't have it in me to be the sort of "jazz hands" type of person who can go for it on demand in a sterile room for a panel of people sitting behind a table.

'I remember auditioning for *Joseph and the Amazing Technicolor Dreamcoat*. This was the biggest musical in the world on tour at the time. I was straight out of Bristol Old Vic Theatre School. Never in my wildest dreams did I imagine I would get the role. Some years earlier, I'd helped Andrew [Lloyd Webber] choose the choir for an earlier production with Jason Donovan. I looked around and every young singer and TV presenter I'd ever seen seemed to be waiting in the wings.

'But then the director, Steven Dexter, asked me to do a monologue, and I was pretty sure most of the others wouldn't have one up their sleeves. I also had to sing "Being Alive", a Sondheim song from his musical, *Company*. I think that helped clinch it. If I'd just gone on stage and sung "Any Dream Will Do", I'm sure I wouldn't have got the part.

'The lesson I learnt from that and other auditioning experiences is to not want the role too much. In other words, you'd like the role, but it's not going to be the end of the world if you don't get it. That way, you might enjoy the process more; you'll certainly be more relaxed, and that's got to help. Easier said than done, I know, but try not to make it the be-all and end-all.'

Ross King – LA correspondent for *Good Morning Britain* and *Lorraine*

'My best advice to anyone auditioning – and I picked this up when I went back to acting classes in Los Angeles – is to make yourself present in the room. Let me explain: I understand why, but invariably people auditioning are nervous; they're thinking about their lines or their lyrics.

'So you need to do three things when you get in front of that panel. It's up to you what they are, but my three start with me looking at the person in the centre of the panel and studying their earlobes. I have very large lobes so I look at theirs in relation to mine. Then I look at my shoes and I give myself a mark between one and ten for how clean and shiny they are. Then I look back at the person on the panel and study their eyebrows to see if they have a mono-brow.

'It's the simplest trick in the world and it works every time. It roots you in that moment and prevents you floating off into a sort of blurred panic. You'll perform better and you'll also put the panel at their ease. They don't want you to communicate your nervousness.

'Also, you need to make a choice. Are you going to come across very big or very small? The answer, of course, is somewhere in the middle. Don't be too cocky but don't be too shy. Show the panel you've got a personality but not one that's going to irritate the hell out of them.

'I'll never forget going to audition for the outrageous, cross-dressing Frank-N-Furter in The Rocky Horror Show, taking over, I hoped, from Jason Donovan. I had to sing, I had to dance – and it seemed to go well.

'When I'd finished my second song, I got lots of encouraging noises.

'Someone then asked when I could start. "Right away!" I said, and as I did so, I dropped my trousers to reveal my legs encased in fishnet stockings. It was a bold choice I'd made in advance but it worked. I was hired on the spot.'

Myleene Klass – singer (Hear'Say), pianist, model and TV and radio presenter

'Before I auditioned for *Popstars* in 2001, I'd been in the West End in *Miss Saigon*. I was then offered the role of Mary Magdalene in *Jesus Christ Superstar*, but when the opportunity of being in Hear'Say came up – much to my father's dismay – I went for the pop option rather than for a guaranteed year on the theatre tour. Luckily, the gamble paid off.

'My experience has shown me the sharp difference between a pop audition and going up for a part in musical theatre. If it's the latter, you'll be reading or singing for a particular role that's already been written and may also have been played already by someone else.

'In the pop world, by contrast, the auditioning panel wants you to play on aspects of your own personality. You'll need a whole different set of skills. At the time of the Hear'Say auditions, I was working as a vocalist on *The Lily Savage Show*, which was something different again.

'Whatever the audition, try not to choose something exceptionally intricate if there's a pianist involved. They might never have seen the music before and they'll only have a few seconds to look over it. I've been on an auditioning panel and watched the pianist being asked to transpose the music up or down a couple of keys. That's so unprofessional. I've also been an audition pianist so I've experienced it at first hand.

'I'd also advise anyone to stay well clear of a particularly popular song that the original singer has made his or her own – unless, that is, you feel you can bring something new to it. Whether they like it or not, there's an imprint in the minds of the panel of how that song sounds. And I wouldn't choose something you've written, however good it might be, because no one will have heard it before.

'As to whether or not you should accompany yourself on piano or guitar, well, it depends on the audition. I'd say no if you're going up for a West End role – there will be an orchestra or band to provide the musical accompaniment. But it can help in a pop audition.

'I'll never forget getting down to the last twenty in the *Popstars* auditions and the pianist was late. I'm classically trained so I sat down and started to play through everyone's pieces with them. One of the judges then walked in and said: "I didn't know you could play the piano." To which I replied: "Well, you didn't ask."

'As to your appearance, my general rule is, if your outfit is louder than you, you've made the wrong decision. So, nothing too outrageous. It's important, too, to show you're adaptable. Think of yourself as being like water that can fill the cracks. But don't try and impersonate Adele or Ed Sheeran or whoever in the way you behave. At all times, remain true to yourself.

'When it comes to nerves, you've got to find a way of dealing with them or they'll start dealing with you – in a negative way. Everybody gets nervous, but the trick is to use them creatively. I'd feel something was wrong, though, if I was waiting to go on stage and I didn't feel nervous. You need that adrenaline to power you onward. If you don't get nervous, you're not taking it seriously.

'I've been on audition panels many times in my career so I have great empathy with anyone who's standing on that spot feeling so isolated and vulnerable. On the other hand, they're being asked to be taken seriously. You wouldn't hand a scalpel to someone just because they fancied being a brain surgeon. The job gets given to the person who you know would do it justice.

'It's one thing to have becoming a singer as your dream but it's no good unless you put in those eight hours a day of practice to prove your ambition is backed up by ability. I don't want to be sitting on a panel wondering whether you'll hit that high note or not, I want to feel that the auditionee is in the driving seat, not that I might have to rescue them in some way.

'I'm still around, sixteen years after being chosen as a Hear'Say band member. Now, I don't profess to be the best or the prettiest or the skinniest or the most talented. What I do think is that I'm a carthorse. If you want those eight bars, I'll have them nailed before we start rehearsing. If you want me to work for four hours, I'll give you five. I'll never show up late and I won't leave first. I'll always give one hundred per cent.

'All of that is just common sense to me. I never forget I'm just a cog in a very big machine. Nobody, absolutely nobody, is irreplaceable. And it's also a good idea to diversify. It's certainly what I've tried to do in my life. As someone once said to me, I'm like a human Swiss Army knife. I can turn my hand to most things.'

Joe McElderry – *The X Factor* winner in 2009

'My first audition ever was for *X Factor* in Manchester. I'd been a big fan of the show from the first series. I was seventeen at the time and absolutely petrified. There must have been about fifty thousand people seated in Old Trafford, hopefuls like me with their families and friends. I was convinced I didn't stand a chance. All around me, people were standing up and rehearsing their songs. But I was much too shy to do that.

'I'd decided to sing Luther Vandross's "Dance with My Father". Over three days, I did three rounds where I sang for the producers and TV executives. And then I heard nothing. That was in the April and I knew the judges' auditions started in the June.

'About a week beforehand, on my eighteenth birthday on 16 June, I was out celebrating with my college friends. I was about to walk into a nightclub when, at ten o'clock at night, my mobile rang. I nearly didn't answer it. But it was one of the show's executives asking me to come back to Manchester the following weekend to sing for the judges.

'I was part of the first time when auditions were held in front of a huge crowd in an arena. Funnily enough, I found it less frightening singing to an audience than in front of four people sitting behind a desk. The pressure is there but you can't see the whites of their eyes in quite the same way.

'Too many people don't embrace their nerves. They try and fight them and that's when you start making mistakes. Nobody has the power to stop their stomach from churning. But if you're nervous, it means you're taking it seriously; your body is producing the adrenaline you need. So go out there and smash it! Channel that excitement, make it work for you.

'You're faced with so many questions before you get to perform. What should I wear? How keen should I seem? In the event, I wore a chequered shirt and jeans with my hair gelled and spiked. I look back now at pictures of me then and I cringe. But that's probably true of any photograph of anyone taken two or five or ten years ago.

'I must have been all right, though, because I kept getting through to the next round. That meant, of course, the pressure increasing each time, not least because people started recognising me in the street, something I wasn't used to and something I hadn't been prepared for. It was instant fame. Suddenly, overnight, I was a TV star. It felt really strange.

'But I come from a very strong family and I was determined to enjoy the experience as much as I could. Cheryl [Cole] was my mentor. There was also a huge team of people ready to give advice if I had any questions. It was a collaborative process. I certainly kept my eyes and ears open to everything that was going on around me. I knew the music industry was a ruthless business; it took me two more years before I really started enjoying myself.

'When I got to the quarter-finals, I started thinking for the first time that I had as much chance as anyone else of going all the way. I didn't think I *would* win, but I did begin to think I *could* win. When it came to the final two, though – me and Olly Murs – I never really believed it would be me. I will never, ever, not for as long as I live, forget the moment when my name was called out. At that moment, my life changed forever.'

Lucy O'Byrne – Runner-up on *The Voice UK* and West End performer

'It sounds like a cliché but just be you. There is no point looking at the people around you when you are sitting outside an audition. You have as much right to be there. Just concentrate on yourself and taking that into the room with you.'

Arlene Phillips – choreographer

'You have to work at everything you do in showbiz – as you do in life. The first thing to do when you walk into a room for an audition is to look like you know what you're doing and deliver what you're being asked to deliver. Easy to say, I know, but you also have to try to hide your nerves.

'I remember working with Michael Crawford once. He was about to embark on a global concert tour, singing the music of Andrew Lloyd Webber. But he'd never used a hand-held microphone. I worked with him eight hours a day, every day, for three weeks, so he could sing with a microphone and look comfortable.

'If you're trying to tell a story – and Michael is a storyteller – you have to think about how you communicate that through the songs and the music. So you don't want your hand tense or shaking because that will detract from what you're trying to put across and prove a distraction to an audience. Nothing comes for nothing in this business. If you want a successful career as a singer, you should never stop listening, never stop learning.'

Paul Potts – *Britain's Got Talent* winner in 2007

'I've had many auditions over the years: two for TV shows but many more for local opera companies and one for an English National Opera Young Artist Programme. They can be like a job interview, but in many ways, they're more exposing. You can often find yourself in a group audition, like I did for the ENO programme, and completely out of your comfort zone, particularly if you're in any way introverted. You might not think that an introvert would be in the entertainment industry but you'd be surprised!

'You also have to listen to your gut. I queued up for *Fame Academy* auditions but ultimately it felt wrong, so in spite of a researcher trying to persuade me to stay, I walked away. If your whole heart isn't in it, the panel and any audience will know.

'As far as the *BGT* audition was concerned, I was surprised to even get the call. I'd flipped a coin to pursue the online application and assumed I wouldn't hear anything. There wasn't a lot of choice in what to wear – all I had was a thirty-five pound suit bought from Tesco that was too small on the chest and too long in the arms.

'I was very nervous before going on, partly because I was uneasy about singing a cappella but also because there was no guarantee that we'd be able to use a backing track.

But my nerves were eased a little when I was told that I could use one after all.

'During the BGT process, I managed my nerves by trying not to think of the next stage until I reached it. Nothing makes you more nervous than anticipation. One thing you have to remember is that nerves never really go away; you just have to find YOUR way of handling them.

'My way frustrates my wife if she's on tour with me. I get ready as late as possible so I have less time to think. I'm someone who can overthink things quite easily, so the less time I have to think, the better. This won't work for everyone, though – you have to learn as much as you can about your own way of doing things.'

Kevin Simm – former member of *Liberty X*, *The Voice UK* winner in 2016

'My first audition was for a school concert when I was fifteen, although I was heavily into football at the time with no real thought that I'd have a career in music one day. I remember being really scared, although when I sang my solo – it was Elton John's "Daniel" – it felt pretty good. My uncle was my role model and he was a good karaoke singer. I wanted to be like him.

'After school, I went to Runshaw College for Performing Arts in Leyland, Lancashire. While I was there, I auditioned for *Stars in Their Eyes* as Simon Fowler from Ocean Colour Scene. I didn't win but it was a really good experience. I was eighteen and it was my first time on television, which meant I was really nervous.

'I still get nervous today before a gig, but now I understand you can use your nerves positively almost to the point where they can help you improve your performance. And I've seen people at auditions with all the confidence in the world, and then they're not that good when it comes to it.

'In 2000, I was in a boy band called Force 5, and we were doing a summer season in Blackpool, singing covers of other people's hits. Our boss at the time sent us for an audition for a talent show which turned out to be *Popstars*. I got to the last ten. The final five were put together as Hear'Say, but the remaining five, including me, decided to form our own band, Liberty X. We lasted six years and had six Top Five hits including a Number One with "Just a Little".

'In 2013, we re-formed for the TV series *The Big Reunion* (Yvie coached us) and then the sold-out arena tour that followed it, which featured other bands that had done well in the early 2000s, like Atomic Kitten, B*Witched and Blue. I'd been gigging in pubs and clubs at the time, so that was a great reminder of what it was like to play for large audiences.

'That whole experience eventually gave me the confidence to audition for *The Voice UK*. The first time I had to sing to those four judges' chairs, their backs turned towards me – and despite everything I'd done up to that point – I was more nervous than I'd ever been in my entire life. There was a lot riding on it for me. I had a bit of a profile, so if no one had turned round, it would have been pretty humiliating. It was a huge gamble which luckily paid off: all four chairs turned!

'As the weeks went on, I didn't get any less nervous, although I was starting to get a lot of support on social media, which gave me a bit of confidence. I only truly believed I could win it when I'd finished singing the very last song on the very last show, even though I'd been the bookies' favourite for quite a little while.'

Shayne Ward – *The X Factor* winner in 2005

'I come from a big Irish family and we've always liked a good sing-song. Then, at sixteen, I joined a band called Destiny. We played in clubs and pubs. I was twenty-one when I went in for *X Factor*, and I had never been more nervous in my entire life than at that first audition. I had hay fever, which didn't help, and one of the songs I had to sing was "You'll Never Get to Heaven" by The Stylistics, which meant hitting a few falsetto notes. But I'd never been taught any technique, and that, along with a large dose of confidence, is what Yvie gave me.

'I must have done all right, though, because I got through to the next round. My nerves didn't get any less as *X Factor* went along, but I did begin to understand how to use them creatively. I never thought I'd win, of course, right up until the end. But I do admit that when I'd finished singing "Somewhere Over the Rainbow" in the final, I thought I might be in with a chance. Again, I have to thank Yvie for coaching me in reaching those high notes and a particularly difficult climbing note that was key to the song and my success in putting it across.

'She also gave me a bit of advice that I've practised to this day. Assuming you've nailed the song, you must imagine you're singing it, she said, not only to a panel of judges and a studio audience but to each individual sitting beyond the cameras at home in front of their television. You must make your song personal to them. When I came off stage, Yvie was there and gave me a big hug. I think it was at that moment everything clicked and I thought that maybe I just might carry off the top prize.'

CHAPTER THIRTEEN

THE ART OF PRESENTATION

WHY FIRST IMPRESSIONS REALLY DO COUNT

Take out that tongue stud! (We'll return to that in a moment.) When you walk into an audition room, you'll be confronted by a panel made up of human beings, all of whom – whether they like to admit it or not – are judgemental. If your personality is so incredible – you're funny, you're friendly – that we love you the minute you stand in front of us, then before you even start singing, we'll want you to do well.

By contrast, if you walk in and you're incredibly annoying – you're cocky, you're obnoxious – we won't like you even before you've sung your first note. Already you'll have put up a barrier. However, we're talking showbiz, so we can kind of forgive someone who's slightly over-enthusiastic, slightly over-confident. Personally, I'd sooner have someone who is a bit over-the-top as opposed to someone who comes in like a little mouse with their head down, without establishing any eye contact. It's much easier to squash, or at least shape, an over-exuberant personality than try to bolster someone who's totally lacking in self-confidence.

You're a performer, so a personality is vitally important. We've all seen people on talent shows who've started out painfully shy but ended up coming out of their shells – we all love to see someone blossoming. So it's important at that very first audition to see just a sliver of your personality, a little slice of potential. As a singer hoping for a long career ahead of them, I'd say personality is almost as important as voice. Having said all that, don't try to be somebody you're not. If you put on a false act of confidence, we'll see through you. The trick, I think, is to believe in yourself. Because if you don't, we won't believe in you. But this is something you can learn, which is why it's very important that you do as many auditions as possible, even for roles or competitions that you're not particularly fanatical about. The fewer you do, the harder you'll try, and that's not always a good thing. We don't want to see desperation written all over your face. I understand why this happens, but people are so fixated on their singing that they walk into a room and panic when they're asked the simplest question. Someone on the panel will almost certainly ask you your name and probably where you're from, what you do for a living or whether you're still at college. It's not rocket science! So have your answers ready in advance.

What we're looking for is likeability. What we don't want is someone so panic-stricken that it's hard to concentrate on their chosen song. That's why it's never a good idea when asked how you're feeling to reply that you're really nervous. Everyone's going to be anxious, but you don't want to signal that to such an extent that the auditioning panel begins to feel uncomfortable. More than that, we'll be expecting you to go wrong.

In the same way, if you've got a cold or a sore throat, don't highlight it before you start singing because then we'll be listening out for it. But if, at the end, you feel you haven't given the best account of yourself because you're under the weather, then do mention it. The key to it all is to project positivity. Start on a negative note and you're in danger of making a rod for your own back; start on a positive one and you're already on the front foot.

A quick word: don't, whatever you do, try and impersonate a particular singer. It's an over-used phrase – and I'm thinking of Louis Walsh here! – but 'make it your own' means what it says. That doesn't mean you should put fancy twirls in every line, but it does mean that the way you phrase a song should sound genuine, as though it means something to you. It will demonstrate that you're not just a karaoke queen (or king).

I cannot emphasise enough the importance of eye contact. Don't single out one person – unless you're wanting to have a bit of a mild flirtation with a particular panellist – but do make sure you look at the panel when you sing. They are your audience, and you won't get very far in this business if you don't look at them.

A lot of people seem to have acquired the habit of singing with their eyes closed. Not a good idea. You can do it once or twice in a song to convey intense emotion, but not all the way through. Connection, connection, connection – nothing's more important.

Obviously, if you make it big, you'll have a stylist who'll advise you how best to dress, what to wear that really suits you. Nobody on an audition panel is expecting you to walk in wearing designer clothes from head to toe. However, there's a big difference between coming along looking scruffy and turning up looking trendy.

I understand that you might be wearing jeans with rips in them because that's the fashion. Personally, I wouldn't wear something like that, but then I'm not trying to break into the music business. And if you've got a quirky style – think of Paloma Faith, for example – then don't be frightened to let us see it. People respond positively to individuals. And it's going to make you much more memorable when we're reviewing the various people who've auditioned at the end of the day.

Turn up in a black T-shirt, black jeans and black boots, and you'd better have a pretty good voice if you're going to make a lasting impression. But your look must be real: don't dress outrageously just for the sake of it.

Whatever your age, whatever your taste, do at least look as though you're clean. If you're doing an audition, don't look as though you haven't washed, as though you haven't made an effort. You need to look like you care. Don't come across as if you couldn't give a s***.

If your ambition is to become an edgy rock star, then by all means, have visible piercings. That said, why on earth would you have a tongue stud if you're asking to be taken seriously as a singer? It may sound obvious, but your tongue is a very important part of your singing. It's a key piece of equipment, if you like.

A stud is going to make your tongue a bit tense. And it will almost certainly make it sound as though you've got a lisp. Why on earth would you want to inhibit the way you sing? It would be like a footballer having a stud in their foot; it would get in the way of them playing the game to the best of their ability. So if you have a tongue stud, take it out before the audition. You can always put it in again as soon as you walk out of the door.

A successful auditionee for me is: someone who's almost certainly auditioned before and who's learnt how to keep their nerves in check; someone who can come across as naturally as possible in what are unnatural circumstances; someone who sings within their capabilities; someone who looks at ease in their own body and their chosen outfit; and someone with the right amount of confidence, who looks the panellists in the eye. All of that might sound blindingly obvious, but you'd be surprised how seldom people get it right.

There's no better example than Leona Lewis. She walked into the room and she was a breath of fresh air. She looked stunning; she performed well; she wasn't too flashy. She wasn't trying too hard either. She wasn't yet the global artist she would become, but you could see enormous potential. I distinctly remember thinking that here was someone who would go far, as she went on to prove.

I still work with Leona from time to time and she's still developing. But then that's true of all major talents. They never just stand still, never just rest on their laurels. They're always keen to hone their talent, to try out different things with their voices.

Talent shows are often criticised, but Leona is a shining vindication of the process, someone who had the raw talent and who, with the right grooming, blossomed into a major artist with a sustained career.

CHAPTER FOURTEEN

HOW TO FIND A SINGING TEACHER

(AND MAKE SURE THEY'RE JUST RIGHT FOR YOU)

I have touched on things you need from a singing teacher all the way through the book, because, obviously, the book is about singing, but here in this chapter are some pointers for what you should specifically look for. This is solely based on my opinion and what I have found to be important down the years. My aim is not to insult any teachers or any specific type of teacher. Every teacher who helps you to feel more confident is worth having. However, out there in the world of singing teaching, you have to search through lots of frogs to find a prince!

Believe me, there are many bluffers in the music business who learn on the job and talk the talk, but there is rather more to it than that. If the worst that happens is that you waste money on going to these people, then so be it, we all learn from our mistakes. Unfortunately, voices can be irreparably damaged through bad teaching. When we trust someone and do whatever they say, it can result in us doing things that aren't comfortable. Even with good teachers, you can have moments where you strain while you are learning, but hopefully most singing teachers will notice and ask you to stop and rest.

So how do you know who is good and who isn't? Firstly, do you want a singing teacher or a vocal coach? Sometimes there isn't much difference, because there is a grey area between the two, but strictly speaking, a singing teacher works on technique and a vocal coach will help you more stylistically. The confusing thing is that many of us call ourselves vocal coaches when we are actually singing teachers, so we don't help matters. Sorry!

I'm actually a singing teacher. On TV shows, I'm always listed in the credits as a vocal coach, so that's why I've started using that title too. Also, people tend to think of singing teachers as classical teachers and vocal coaches as pop teachers, which isn't necessarily the case. As I said, it's a grey area. The best thing is just to speak to the teacher or coach in question and find out what they do. What you want ideally is a cross between the two. You want someone who has a great knowledge of vocal technique and will help you to actually improve and look after your instrument (by that I mean your voice, of course!) but who will also understand the type of music you sing. There's no point in having a fabulous technical teacher who teaches you to sound like a choirboy or a musical theatre singer if you want a pop career. However, just because their background may be MT (musical theatre) or classical, that doesn't mean they haven't learnt how to work with pop singers – so find out who they work with and look at the results, or try to chat to other students about this.

Technique is the be-all and end-all when it comes to teaching, but a good teacher should help you to still sound like you, unless what you are doing is totally dangerous and detrimental to your voice.

When I was in my final year at singing college in my late twenties (yes, it takes many years to train as an opera singer), I started to teach some of the dance and drama students. I thought I would automatically be able to teach because I had studied for so long, but when I look back now, I realise I was dreadful. It takes years of teaching to become good at it, because to begin with it's trial and error as to what works for other people and what way of explaining it works best. Now I'm not saying that you should therefore only work with teachers who are older but what I am saying is that if you feel that your teacher is bluffing and doesn't know much more than you do yourself, politely move on to someone more experienced.

I have seen a couple of examples of people straight out of college who have landed great teaching jobs, and I have witnessed some of the horrendous teaching they do. They get away with it either because the students are good anyway or because they don't know any better.

If the teacher keeps saying, 'Wow, you have improved so much!' then it's easy to be taken in by it, and in a way you probably will improve because that will make you more confident. But beware!

I have many stories from singers that I can't repeat here! I've known singers who have gone to lessons with coaches with huge names on their CVs, only to find that those coaches knew less than they did. So beware of people who have just been in the right place at the right time. Even though I've taught some big names and have appeared on TV, I still want the people who come to me not to be afraid to question me if I talk rubbish.

Of course, it's not just young teachers who can be dangerous. Some teachers have been getting away with the bluffing for years. I'm not trying to scare you off; I just want to warn you not to be afraid to ask questions and not to accept advice from a teacher that feels wrong. So which assets do I suggest you look for in a teacher?

- Personally, I wouldn't want to work with someone who couldn't play the piano at all. I like to rehearse with my singing teacher and go through my songs, some of which are in sheet music form. Also, if tracks aren't in the correct key, it's good to try the melody up or down a tone, for example, and that's something that can be tried out with the help of the piano.

  And doing vocal exercises in a key to suit each student is vital.

  A teacher doesn't have to be brilliant on the piano (my own playing needs a bit of practise now and then!) but I think knowledge of the keyboard is vital for understanding exactly where each student's range sits.

- I would want to know that my teacher had sung at some reasonable level themselves, and therefore really understands singers and can demonstrate that to a certain degree. Obviously, all singing teachers can't hit every note in every key, but they should be able to give you an idea of what they can do.

- You need to like your teacher and not be afraid of them. It's good to have a bit of teacher/ pupil respect, but you shouldn't think of them as being like a schoolteacher who is unapproachable. This is the person whom you need to be the most comfortable with vocally. It's the person who should see you at your best and at your worst.

  I always get very attached to my students and I think it's mutual. They text me if they are worried about something, and sometimes they have a cry in lessons if we are working on an emotional song. When you come to a singing lesson, you can't leave your emotions at home. Your voice is part of you. In order to sing well, you have to open up and bare your soul. You have to be prepared to make a fool of yourself or to crack a note. It doesn't matter which horrendous versions of songs your teacher hears, singing lessons should be a bit like Vegas: what happens in the lesson stays in the lesson!

  A good relationship with your teacher is one where you don't have to come in and put on an act.

- Ask yourself: does what they are telling me to do feel right? Sometimes it can take a couple of lessons to understand why you are doing certain exercises, and even if the teacher explains it all, it can take a while to see an improvement. But don't beat yourself up! Different voices take different amounts of time to see a change. However, if what you are being asked to do just feels wrong or it hurts, ask the teacher to explain it all again.

  It should never hurt to sing.

  Your voice can get tired while the muscles are dealing with new ideas, and your voice can get tired while learning new songs because the muscles aren't prepared for which notes they are going to hit...

  But it shouldn't hurt.

  If it hurts, tell the teacher, and if things don't change, you should perhaps have a lesson with someone else and see if they explain things to you better. As a teacher, I wouldn't want someone to persevere with me if they weren't happy. However, I wouldn't want them just to leave without explaining what they didn't understand.

  So talk to your teacher; you won't be the first one to ask questions. Good teachers want you to be able to ask them things as many times as you need to. Most teachers genuinely want each and every student to feel happy and at ease.

- How do you know if you have a bluffer, as I talked about earlier? As a professional singer, you need to be knowledgeable about the voice. You should be reading about vocal technique, listening to singers, talking technique with other singers, watching singers and seeing who does what. Unfortunately, some singers in the charts aren't always the best examples of good technique, but gradually you will see who strains and who doesn't.

The more knowledge you have yourself, the easier it will be for you to see if your teacher is actually helping you to improve. If you feel you are wasting your money, I wouldn't suggest abandoning lessons altogether. As a singer, you constantly need that extra pair of ears, and remember, we don't hear our voices the way others hear them. In this case, I would suggest you find another teacher. If they are more expensive, just go once a month instead of weekly, but still go to lessons. Having constant singing lessons is vital at all stages of your career if you really care about your voice.

I still have lessons with my good friend Graeme Lauren, who has the same background in technique as I have. It's not because I don't know things that I need lessons, it's because I forget to do the things I should, I get lazy vocally, or I just don't realise that I have started getting into bad habits.

As a singer, your voice constantly changes and you need to be monitoring those changes if you want to keep on singing well. Think again of Andy Murray – he can play tennis! There isn't a thing about tennis he doesn't know, but in order to play at his absolute best and not get into any bad habits, he still has his coaching. I work with singers who, like Andy, are at the very top of their game, but they still come into their lessons like everyone else, eager to learn and full of insecurities.

The singer's psyche is an incredible juxtaposition of ego fighting against insecurity. We all feel on top of the world when we are singing well, but equally, a bad singing day or a bad performance – or even just not hitting one note – can send us into the depths of despair.

- Following on from what we have just been discussing, going to a good singing teacher is a bit like visiting a 'shrink'. Aside from what you have learnt in the lesson, do you feel better when you leave your lessons or do you feel a bit down because you didn't achieve what they were trying to teach you?

  Singing teachers often have to get inside your head and find the 'thing' that is preventing you from hitting a certain note or being able to sing a certain phrase. Sometimes it's not a technical fault or a lack of technical knowledge, but an emotional or psychological barrier you are putting up.

  A singing teacher is like a doctor. Sometimes it's obvious to the doctor what your problem is; other times they need to delve deeper and get you to open up about all your symptoms, not just the obvious ones. We get great doctors who just seem to care more and understand you more, and it's exactly the same with singing teachers.

The best teachers have enough patience and insight to know the whole you.

- The final piece of the puzzle in finding a singing teacher who is right for you is the structure of the lessons. Ideally your teacher should work on some technical exercises for the first half of each lesson and then move on to working on songs. This can, of course, vary depending on your requirements. If you are a complete beginner, you might spend whole lessons on technique, and if you are very experienced, you might warm up at home or be able to do your exercises yourself. Maybe you just want to concentrate on certain songs you have to perfect.

These are just guidelines. As long as you are both happy with the structure, there is no set rule. However, if you are spending whole lessons on exercises and you want to work on songs, talk to your teacher. Being happy with the structure of each lesson is important, because if you pay for an hour's tuition, you want to achieve what you have come for during that time.

I've been told that some teachers talk so much during lessons that not much singing gets done at all! If that is the case in your lessons, maybe point out in a jokey way that you both talked too much last time so your aim today is to actually sing for an hour, and perhaps they will get the hint.

To summarise...

- Finding a teacher who is right for you is very personal.
- The so-called 'best' teacher who is constantly busy might be someone you just don't click with.
- Remember, it's your money: they are working for you, not vice versa.
- Have the courage to say what you want or find someone else.
- Most people kiss a lot of frogs before they find their prince!

CHAPTER FIFTEEN

COMPLEMENTARY THERAPIES

(AND WHY WE MIGHT NEED THEM)

There are exceptions to every rule. We teach our children that if they behave perfectly, are dedicated and work hard, they will achieve more in life. That's certainly true. In most cases, the harder you work and the more dedicated you are, the more successful you'll be. However, with singing, we know of quite a few exceptions. We know that above all, it's about your talent, and that there are some singers out there who have been lucky. They've not necessarily put in the work or looked after their voices as they should, but their success has been incredible. Just remember, though, that they are the exceptions. Don't for a minute think that you'll just be lucky and suddenly a singing career will fall into place for you.

I'd say that 99.9 per cent of successful artists have succeeded by a combination of incredible dedication, passion and workload. They will have gigged in places you wouldn't even want to have a night out in. Those on stage will have done many unsuccessful and often soul-destroying auditions before landing a part. The successful songwriters will have written dozens of songs they've had to bin. (I'd love to root around in the bins of Ed Sheeran, Adele or Sam Smith!)

I make a living from teaching singing, but a lot of my bills have been paid by TV talent shows, so I'd be the last one to criticise them. However, if they have a fault, it's making a generation of young singers believe that they don't have to do the hard graft, they can just turn up and they'll become stars overnight. In reality, even those people lucky enough to do well in these shows have to work their socks off. In fact, when you make it big in a TV show, you're almost immediately subjected to people calling you a one-hit wonder and making jokes about you returning to your day job.

Believe me, when you sign a record deal, before the champagne glasses have even been washed up, you'll be in a car heading to a rehearsal or having an early night before a flight at seven in the morning. Record companies don't just throw money at people and expect them to sit back and wallow in the glory, quite the contrary. They have huge overheads themselves. The success of your album will pay the wages of their many employees, so if you don't work hard, you'll be dropped almost before you've had time to wheel your new Louis Vuitton luggage off the plane.

The public buy into the lavish lifestyles of the stars: they want to be them. They fancy waking up in Malibu and partying in Vegas. They want the designer clothes and the screaming fans. What they don't want to know about is the fact you've had three hours' sleep, you haven't seen your family for a month and you've had ten hours of rehearsals every single day this week. We don't hear about the tough side of being a star; we only see the burnout when it all gets too much, and we don't really understand why. What I'm saying is, don't be fooled. What you're getting into has incredible rewards and incredible highs like no other job, but it's also one of the hardest careers you can pick.

If you don't put the work in now, it won't happen. Once it does, you need to keep it up or it will fall apart. In other words, you'd better get your work ethic sorted out now and prepare yourself for a marathon.

If that all sounds like too much scaremongering, here's a way to make it achievable...

Your voice is contained inside your body. From the muscles in your throat to the emotions in your head, you control everything that comes out. So how do you make sure you're consistently good? It can't just be about exercising the muscles, because when we're feeling sad, it's pretty impossible to summon up the energy to perform a joyful song.

As a singer, you have to realise that the whole of you is important. So let's take a look at your health and wellbeing, your mental state, your confidence, your resilience and your expectations. There's no point in making it big and then falling at the first hurdle because you're unprepared and lacking in confidence.

Let's talk about all the possible things that can help you

as a whole. If you have the time and the money to do all of these, that's great; some of you, however, could just read about them and understand enough. Others might go to a couple of classes to get the basics and that will be all they need. Let's explore them all, anyway.

In this book, we are attacking that singing career of yours with everything we've got. It's a case of: 'I'm giving it my all, and if it doesn't work out, I'll have no regrets.' That's the attitude I see time and time again in very successful artists. So here are some things which might complement or improve your lifestyle as a singer:

Alexander Technique

I first came across the Alexander Technique as a young student at music college while studying piano. My teacher was a very tall, lanky man who sort of floated around. When he walked up stairs, he looked like he was on an escalator, and when he played the piano, it was as if his hands belonged to someone else. He had a lack of tension that I'd never seen in anyone before.

He explained to me that he was a great believer in the Alexander Technique, and he sent me to some classes to help relieve tension when I was practising Chopin nocturnes or Mozart sonatas. It became second nature to me to carry myself in the way I'd been taught in these Alexander Technique classes, and it wasn't until some time later that I realised how much it helped my singing.

I am no Alexander Technique expert, because it has been a great many years since I had classes, but even though it was a long time ago, it's something that I've never forgotten and feel could be of use to everyone.

The basic principle of the Alexander Technique is to become aware of bad postural habits we've picked up, and how we develop tensions that we don't need when we get stressed or do everyday tasks. The Alexander Technique teaches us how to re-learn a natural balance in our bodies, which, in my opinion, is health-giving and extremely useful for any performer for whom the show has to go on, no matter how stressed they are that day.

Find out a bit about the Alexander Technique via the Internet or try a class out to see if you find it helpful. It's certainly something I would recommend.

Yoga

I have dabbled a tiny bit in yoga but it's now something I intend to take up properly. I need to find the time (maybe when I've finished writing this book)!

Many performers benefit from yoga. Posture is very important in yoga and also in singing. Breathing is a big part of yoga classes, so again there is a connection.

My good friend, Rosie Wright, is a fantastic example of practising what you preach. Rosie lectures in yoga and has taught many classes. She also loves singing in her spare time. Her posture is fantastic. She always looks serene and well-balanced, and has an air of calm. As a singer, you'd do well to have Rosie's posture, so I've asked her to tell us exactly what yoga involves and why it would be beneficial to singers.

Here is Rosie's advice: 'One of the great wonders of yoga is how practising it can affect many aspects of your life – for the better! It is now recognised that establishing a yoga practice helps the body to be flexible and strong. In the process, it also has a similarly positive effect on the voice.

'By practising a mixture of breathing (pranayama) and postures (asana), you can find space and support for your voice within. This is a tremendous advantage, since it means that your vocal instrument is housed well and support can be found freely from the diaphragm.

'The other great advantage is that yoga helps the nervous system be calm and steady. The focus and self-confidence that yoga nurtures is really vital for pre-performance jitters.

'I discovered yoga as a student in my teens and immediately realised how it helped my singing in a choir and kept me calm and focused during a performance.

'I trained to become a yoga teacher and have been teaching yoga for many years. Check out the British Wheel of Yoga for classes near you.'

Pilates

Pilates classes aim to improve your general fitness and core strength. Many people find Pilates very useful for singing. It concentrates on posture and getting rid of unnecessary tensions in the body; it also concentrates on working the abdominal muscles, which are, of course, very important in singing. However, I would be mindful of the fact that in

Pilates, there's often a lot of emphasis on pulling the tummy towards the spine, which is great, although for singing, we must also be able to release those same muscles in order to breathe efficiently.

I sometimes have problems with singers who spend a lot of time either at Pilates classes or in the gym pulling in their abdominal muscles. The 'fat' that I talk about in my teaching of diaphragmatic breathing (see also page 64) has to be possible, too. If you pull your tummy muscles in, that's good, as long as for singing you're able to let them go again. Dancers can also be guilty of this – they spend a lot of time pulling their tummies in but not letting them out again. By all means get all the benefits of Pilates, but just be aware of this one thing.

Gym Work

Any exercise you can do as a singer will hopefully be beneficial. As I've explained earlier, looking after your whole body and mind will help your singing voice. However, be mindful of the fact that working in the gym with heavy weights – especially if unsupervised – can cause you tension, especially in the shoulders, neck and jaw.

Speak to a trainer at the gym about the way you do your exercises or the way you lift your weights. Explain that you're a singer so you need to keep a balance between being tight and being relaxed. We do need a certain amount of muscle power and tension, but it has to be in the correct muscles. Unnecessary tension is detrimental to a singer and can result in forced singing. Speak to someone who knows about working specific muscles beforehand. Don't just go into the gym and guess what to do. A trainer should be able to write a programme for you and review it now and then, making sure you are continuing to do the exercises or use the equipment correctly and safely.

Aerobic Work

I'm a runner, and I definitely believe that my singing is better as a result. I try to run most days of the week. Sometimes, of course, I just pull the covers up over my head and have half an hour more sleep, but generally I get out there and do something.

I don't like going to the gym, I like running in the fresh air. I arrange to meet friends every morning, so I have to go through the embarrassment of cancelling if I'm feeling lazy. In order not to let my friends down, I usually end up going, and even on days when I haven't felt like it, I always feel energised and positive afterwards.

Aerobic exercise is great for our breathing. It also helps to release endorphins, a group of hormones secreted within the brain and the nervous system. They're often called feel-good hormones because they create a euphoric state. When we feel positive at the start of the day, we're much more likely to achieve more in our singing practice. And as I keep saying, when you work on your voice with your whole body and mind, you get great results.

I may be imagining it, but when I start the day with a run, I certainly feel like I'm singing better. On the other hand, when I haven't run for a few days because I've been too busy, I feel a bit lethargic and fed up, and my singing voice seems to feel the same.

Of course, there are other forms of exercise that may work better for you, perhaps spin classes or aerobics if you prefer to exercise with other people. I'm just talking about running because that's my passion. Any exercise that gets your muscles working and your heart beating faster is great. We all know of exceptions, but in general, being fit is so important for your singing.

The added bonus in doing any sort of exercise is that we'll probably look better. Perhaps slimmer, perhaps more toned, but people who are energised and active always look better in my opinion than couch potatoes, although I'm certainly guilty of being one of those from time to time.

As a singer, how you look is important. I would be lying to say it isn't. I'm certainly not saying you can't make it if you're overweight, that would be ridiculous. Some of the most gorgeous people I know are a bit curvy, but it's all about being the best 'you' that you can be. Surely we need to tick as many boxes as we can and give ourselves the biggest chance of success possible? If being a bit more disciplined about what we eat and how much exercise we do means we get the jobs we want, then it must be worth it.

Pavarotti wasn't a shining example of a man chosen for his six-pack, but unfortunately, not many of us are blessed with a talent like his – most of the rest of us have to work that bit harder.

Dance

It is by no means essential that every singer should be able to dance, and often the tight abdominal muscles that dancers use can make it difficult to release the tummy when practising diaphragmatic breathing (see also page 64). However, as long as dancers practise this release, most of them have excellent posture, which is always an advantage.

Being able to carry yourself well on stage is something that dance can help with. Also, from a fitness point of view, dancing is a great way for singers to improve both their performance skills and their aerobic capacity at the same time. These two disciplines, dancing and singing, often complement each other.

It's no longer acceptable for singers in almost any genre to look wooden on stage. If two singers audition for a role, the one with the slightly better voice may be pipped at the post by the one who just seems more at ease with their performance skills. Going to some movement or dance classes can certainly help with this. Equally, many dancers have to be able to sing when they go to certain stage auditions.

Jacquie Storey, an eminent choreographer, says: 'To be a versatile working dancer within the industry, a strong dance technique, alongside an understanding of vocal technique, will support all styles of work and give the performer the stamina required as a working artist.

'For those dancers who want to cast the net wider as far as types of auditions are concerned, it is no longer acceptable to simply be able to "hold the melody" or "belt out a tune". A much higher standard is required in these days of incredibly fierce competition.'

Therefore, as a singer, why wouldn't you have a similar attitude? Get yourself some dance or movement skills, which can only add to your talents; you never know: it might be the difference between you or another singer getting a particular job.

Hypnotherapy

This may sound a bit scary, and it's certainly a complementary therapy rather than a necessity. Most singers can get over stage fright through gaining confidence and just exposing themselves to more performing, but for those who still really struggle, hypnosis is not as crazy a suggestion as it may sound.

I myself am a confident person in many ways. I've done many live TV shows and loved the excitement of it! However, when it comes to singing, I've always found it scary – I start thinking I'm going to forget my words or just forget the song altogether.

I went for hypnosis and didn't feel like anything happened at all. I'm sure I didn't fall asleep or go 'under his spell'. And yet, somehow, my next performance was so different. I was more excited than scared and I actually enjoyed it. I've never looked back, and if I had something big coming up, I'd go again.

I'm not suggesting you all try hypnotherapy, I'm just saying that whatever you feel would help you as a singer, give it a go. Again, it's important to ask around and maybe go to someone that a friend or another performer has used. I went to someone who has helped a lot of actors.

Standing on a stage on your own in front of hundreds of people may come easily to some people, while others, no matter how talented they are, find it daunting. Like me, you might find that it's the final piece missing from the puzzle.

Laryngeal Manual Therapy or Massage

When singers or voice users of any sort present with symptoms such as losing part of their range, a breathy tone, unexpected vocal fatigue or more difficulty in dealing with the *passaggio* than usual, the first thing most of us voice teachers would do would be to send that person to an ENT (ear, nose and throat) specialist. However, as a first port of call, a visit to a physiotherapist who specialises in dealing with voice users might be a good idea.

Ed Blake, better known in the business as 'Physio Ed', is one of the top experts in his field and has a clinic in London's Harley Street. He explained to me what he does.

'I tend to call what I do laryngeal manual therapy rather than massage, because it's not just soft tissue work. It targets the soft tissue but it also targets the joints of the larynx as well.

'We want to see if the problems are caused by muscular restrictions or tensions. I target tight muscles in an aim to restore efficient movement. The aim is to release tight musculature to allow the mechanism to move normally again. This works from the principle that if it WORKS the way it was designed to, chances are it will BEHAVE the way it was designed to.'

Ed says that the results are usually pretty instantaneous, with significant improvement generally seen after one or two sessions. However, if the symptoms are largely unchanged after visiting him twice, his advice would be to go to an ENT specialist to rule out any possible structural cause.

The sorts of people who visit Ed are any voice users at all, from teachers to call-centre workers to barristers to rock, pop and classical singers. Ed says there are many causes for these 'tensions'. It could be poor technique, a crazy workload or sometimes illness. Often poor posture is to blame. Through laryngeal manual therapy, Ed will reset everything properly, and then it's up to the singer to maintain this set-up as best they can, through paying attention to their technique, posture and workload, if at all possible.

If poor posture or tension is causing head, neck and shoulder discomfort, and not necessarily vocal problems, any good physiotherapist or massage therapist will be able to help. It's sometimes good to nip this tension in the bud before it leads to problems with your voice.

Rebecca Kier, a chartered physiotherapist working in the musculoskeletal field, says poor posture and weakness of the core muscles can be major factors in the cause of tension in the head, neck and shoulder areas, further adding to problems.

All chartered physiotherapists must be registered with the Health and Care Professions Council (HCPC) in order to practise. The HCPC is our governing body and serves as a regulator set up to protect the public; it keeps a register of health and care professionals who meet its standards for training, professional skills, behaviour and health.

You can find a chartered physiotherapist with the necessary skills by contacting:-

The Chartered Society of Physiotherapy (CSP): http://www.csp.org.uk/

The Health and Care Professions Council (HCPC): http://www.hcpc-uk.co.uk/

CHAPTER SIXTEEN

THE TEAM AROUND YOU

I'm back to my comparisons with athletes and singers. In the same way that an athlete needs a team behind him or her, so does a singer. When we embark on a career as a singer, we need psychological back-up as well as people to look after our practical needs.

Obviously it depends what stage of your career you are at as to whether you have a big entourage or not. We sometimes laugh at stars turning up with the entourage in tow, but it makes life so much easier for the singer when everyone has specific jobs.

As someone who may well be starting out on their career, you don't, of course, need to immediately employ a large team. But on a much smaller scale, you do still need to find key people who can support you in this venture.

Singing Teacher

First, of course, you'll need a singing teacher (see also Chapter Fourteen). While first and foremost, the technical knowledge of your singing teacher is absolutely essential, it's also very important that you like this person and trust them enough to bare your soul to them. Singing is so personal, so emotional, that at some points in your lessons you'll have to strip away all barriers and false confidence, and often tears will be shed.

As an opera student, I had intensive drama lessons with a wonderful man called Patrick Libby. He made us shout, cry, strip off, laugh and search deep inside ourselves for every emotion we could find. It was hard going on many days, but until I worked with Patrick, I didn't understand how to convey different emotions while performing. He saw us at our best and our worst but we trusted him, and to this day, if I need to search for an emotion while performing, I use the techniques he taught me. I've been able to help many of my singers find that extra something while performing thanks to Patrick.

If you really want to get the best out of your singing lessons, you need to find someone in front of whom you have no inhibitions, so you can take risks, try higher notes and be brave in a way you perhaps couldn't be outside those four walls.

(Don't worry: the stripping-off bit was something we did as actors! Sometimes actors need to do intimate scenes and the like. Not so vital for most singers, although mind you, modern opera productions demand all sorts nowadays. But that's another story!)

I suppose what I'm really saying is that your singing teacher should also be a real mentor to you.

When I'm with one of my singers who has a particular worry about a specific performance, I always say the same thing to them: 'Hand over all the worrying to me. You just tell me all your worries and totally trust me to sort them out, whether it's a vocal problem or a practical one. Now all you have to do is stand up there and sing.'

Of course, if your teacher is wonderful in every way but you don't see them as a mentor, you could look elsewhere for that back-up. Perhaps you have someone you look up to who could help you with your career and be a mentor to you. It doesn't need to be a singer, just someone who understands the business and can be supportive to you: having someone in whom you can confide your worries is important.

Most singers have insecurities and worries about their voices. I've always believed it's harder than playing the piano or the drums. Your voice is part of you. If you feel sad, it's hard to sing a happy song. If you have a sore throat, you don't want to sound like you're moaning and you don't want to let down your audience, but you can't be sure what your voice will sound like and you don't want to damage it. You need someone who can understand all these problems and provide a shoulder to lean on when you need it.

In the team of people around you, the most important one is arguably your singing teacher.

Performance Coaching

When you're ready to perform, you need someone who can help you with performance. It all depends on your budget. If you're earning good money from singing, it's worth paying for someone to help you hone your performance. However, if you're just starting out, see if it's something your singing teacher is also good at; alternatively, it might be worth booking one session with a performance coach or a choreographer who specialises in working with singers on performance, not just dance.

Many singing teachers who have been performers themselves are great at this. Choreographers who understand that singers need help with how to portray emotions (and even how to walk across the stage without looking awkward) can be a great help too. Don't be fooled into thinking that choreographers only teach dance routines. I work with many amazing choreographers who teach the singers to do LESS on stage rather than more.

Rehearsal Pianist or Musical Director

Again, budgetary requirements are important, but depending on whether you sing to ready-made tracks or work with a live band, you need to get to know some musicians. Knowing a great keyboard player or a musical director (MD), who can help you to make your own tracks or rehearse with you while playing the piano, can be really helpful. They can do what is called 'routining'. This is when they rehearse your songs with you in the key that suits you best and edit them to the lengths you need. Often they also have knowledge of how to make new tracks that are better suited to you than just a karaoke version. We talked before about making the song your own. If a track is made to suit you, this can really help create your version of the song.

If you're a musical theatre singer or a classical singer, it's even more essential that you work with a great pianist, who can rehearse with you and get to know your voice. (In opera, we call them 'répétiteurs' and they're as important for coaching you as your singing teacher.)

Stylist

While a stylist is brilliant for busy singers who have to rush from TV shows to gigs, until you have high earnings, it's not an essential and therefore not something you need early on in your career. It is, however, a good idea to start to develop a style of your own, whatever that may be, and stick to it. It's like your signature: something that people get to know as part of you.

Don't just wear what's in fashion; really think about having your own look. By that, I don't necessarily mean anything crazy; just have a bit of a theme that expresses who you are. If you can't afford a stylist, you could try and team up with a young designer or fashion student who could help you to create something special. I know lots of singers who do this.

Management

Do I need a manager? It's a question I'm often asked by singers. In the singing world, managers and agents are often separate people, although sometimes they perform both roles. Agents book gigs for singers, and it's always good to be on their books. You will pay them a percentage of your fee for each gig, but without them, you probably wouldn't get the gigs in the first place.

A good manager works on your career from every angle. Again, you would only pay them a percentage of your fees from gigs you get through them, but even when they aren't getting you gigs, they would still be doing other things for you, like setting up meetings with record companies or having ideas as to how you could run your career. So these things would essentially be done for free.

A manager who takes on young singers usually doesn't mind that they're working for free for a while, because if they believe in you and your career takes off, they'll earn a percentage of all the money you earn if you're successful. It's also flattering to think that they obviously believe in you enough to invest in you.

It's important that if your manager is with you at the start and helps you get a foot up into the business, you don't then leave them as soon as you're successful: aim for integrity in your career.

Louis Walsh is a great example of a manager. He always teaches his singers to be respectful and hard-working, because people remember that and are more likely to rebook them. Performers who act like divas in front of anyone who they think isn't important, like the runners and the assistants, get a shock when years later those people are running the show and remember their rudeness. They always say in the music business, BE NICE TO THE PEOPLE ON THE WAY UP BECAUSE YOU WILL NEED THEM ON YOUR WAY DOWN. Undoubtedly, a career in the music business can have many ups and downs, but never get above your station. Remember, just because you're the so-called star at the front of the stage, you're no more important to the gig than the person working your spotlight. Without them doing their job properly, you'll look like a fool.

BE NICE! YOU'RE VERY LUCKY TO BE DOING WHAT YOU'RE DOING.

I remember being in a room with a singer, who will remain nameless, who was berating everyone present for being in a bad mood. What the singer didn't realise was that before they'd arrived, everyone had been laughing and joking. It was their arrival that had dampened the mood because we'd all known what was coming.

Don't be that person who people talk about.

I've encountered many divas in my time – like the female singer who told me to f*** off so many times that one day I shouted it back and left her to it! On another occasion, I was working with a band and when we walked on set almost every member of the crew said: 'Oh no, not them!' Their diva reputation was legendary. They spoke to me like I was of no use to them at all (it was someone else who booked me on their behalf), so I was secretly quite glad when I realised they were divas to everyone and it wasn't just me.

Also, I've turned up in different countries of the world to work with singers who 'just don't feel like it today'. (It doesn't bother me, I still get paid!)

On the other hand, when I was rehearsing for that legendary *X Factor* duet with Alexandra Burke and Beyoncé, who could justifiably have been the biggest diva ever, she was just the opposite. I was reminding Alexandra of some technical things on stage, when Beyoncé suddenly said: 'Oh, please can you help me with that, too?'

Another huge star I worked with who was unbelievably normal was the wonderful Hollywood actress Glenn Close. We'd been working together at her home for a while, so we knew each other quite well by this stage. On this particular day, we were recording at the famous Capitol Studios in LA. We had a really long lunch break, so we decided to head to my hotel, The Sunset Tower, for lunch.

She got into my rental car with me, which was a convertible. We put the roof down and we sang through all the songs from all the shows we could think of at the tops of our voices. I remember driving down Sunset Boulevard, thinking I must be in a dream! Proof indeed that singing makes you happy, whether you're a Hollywood superstar or an ordinary person.

Glenn Close is one of the best examples of not having to be a diva to be successful. But then real stars are seldom the biggest divas. It will do you no harm to always remember that.

We're all human and we all have a strop sometimes when things get too pressured, but always apologise, never take yourself so seriously that you can't laugh at yourself when you've been a bit diva-like, and you won't go far wrong. A good team around you will keep you grounded. Ideally, if you find a good team at the beginning, you'll be able to keep many of them with you throughout your career.

Throat Specialist

Hopefully, you'll never need to consult an ENT specialist, but if singing is your career, having a check-up every now and then, or having someone you trust who can fit you in when you're in danger of having to cancel a very important gig, is probably sensible.

In the early days, if you're worried about your throat, go to your GP. Explain that your voice is your living and you're concerned. Your GP will do a superficial examination and will be able to tell a lot from your speaking voice. If they're concerned, they will hopefully either give you some medication to try or refer you to a specialist.

The first port of call is often a medication called lansoprazole; this helps alleviate the symptoms of acid reflux, which we discussed in Chapter Three on vocal hygiene (see also pages 26-27). I'm not a doctor so I cannot recommend that you ask for this, but it's certainly something you could discuss with your GP. I've often sat in on consultations with singers and throat specialists, and this is what I've seen prescribed time after time. So if your doctor thinks it's appropriate for you, then perhaps it's a good place to start.

If your doctor recommends that you see a specialist, the waiting time might be quite long on the NHS. If you feel that it's important you see a specialist as soon as possible, ask your GP the name of the specialist they were sending you to, and you can perhaps try to see them privately. Again, I don't know your budget, but if you're working as a singer, you have to weigh up potential missed earnings from cancelled gigs against how much you'll have to pay to go privately.

Assuming you have a rapport with this throat specialist, if and when you see them, store their number in your phone and say you'd like to use them again, if possible. Try to build up a relationship where they would fit you in if you had a vocal emergency (a lost voice before a big gig, for example).

Of course, if you're going privately, you can choose who you see, and it's a good idea to consult someone who specialises in singers. Perhaps your singing teacher can recommend someone, or maybe there's a singer you know who's been to a particular specialist before. Ask around – word-of-mouth recommendations are usually really good.

I have a small list of wonderful specialists near me whom I've used for all my singers, whether they're international superstars or people starting out on their careers. They get the same treatment and the same reassurance.

In the early days of my career, I went to see a throat specialist more often, because I didn't know my own voice as well as I do now and I worried about it more. My wonderful throat doctor, Ardeshir Khambata (or 'Eddie', as we all knew him), was a very important part of this 'team' that I'm telling you we all need. I could contact Eddie if I was concerned, and he always gave me great advice and support. He had studied singing himself, which made his understanding of the voice, and more importantly, a singer's psyche, second to none.

Sadly, Eddie is no longer with us, but try to find yourself an Eddie. There are many devoted laryngologists out there who love the job they do.

A Word from the Doctor

Voice production is a complicated business, and understanding the workings of your voice as well as you can, so that you can avoid injury, is vitally important. However, I am no doctor, so I've asked one of the most eminent throat doctors in the UK to write a bit of an explanation for you.

John Rubin, MD FACS FRCS, is a consultant ENT surgeon at UCLH and is lead clinician for voice disorders at the Royal National Throat, Nose and Ear Hospital in London. He is an honorary consultant ENT surgeon at the National Hospital for Neurology and Neurosurgery, an honorary visiting professor at City, University of London, and an honorary senior lecturer at University College London.

Here is what he has to say: 'All of us rely on our voice. We expect that it will be available to us, at a moment's notice, that it will be effortless and that it will accomplish what we ask of it. Yet voicing is the end product of a surprising number of seemingly disparate parts of our body. The idea of what we wish to say begins in our brain in parts of our cortex still being mapped with modern technology, such as functional magnetic resonance imaging (fMRI). The sub-cortex, the messenger part of our brain, is actively involved. Depending on the degree of emotional content in the vocal message, the midbrain will be activated to a greater or lesser degree.

'Our brainstem, including areas integral to life itself (for example, the area that controls respiration), is stimulated, and a large series of messages are sent to muscles in our lips, face, tongue and abdominal and chest walls, just to name a few peripheral areas.

'The cervical nerve rootlets involved in respiration are activated and instruct our diaphragm to contract, thereby causing a sudden expansion of our thoracic cage and the intake of breath, at the same moment that the muscles controlling our vocal cords are instructed to open. Our laryngeal muscles are then instructed to tense, stretch and bring the vocal cords back to a position of near-complete closure at the same time that the abdominal muscles contract and the diaphragm starts to relax. Air is released from the lungs in a controlled fashion and sent cephalad (upwards) through our trachea, towards our vocal folds (cords), the streams of air caressing the vocal folds and causing them to vibrate.

'The fundamental frequency, and thus the underlying sound, of our voice, depends on the number of times per second that the vocal folds vibrate. This in turn is dependent on the tension and stretch being placed on them as well as the pressure placed against them from below. For example, if you "decide" that you wish to create a sound of a 440 (A4 or Stuttgart pitch [440 Hz]), you will "instruct" your muscles around the vocal folds to put the exact amount of tension required to make them vibrate 440 times per second. This is obviously something that can be "learnt".

'The vocal fold vibrations, and there may be hundreds per second[1], send an equivalent number of pulses of air up towards the lips. These pulses are shaped by the structures that they meet – the epiglottis, the base of the tongue, pharyngeal walls, soft palate, cheeks and lips. Some of the sound pulses produced are absorbed (damped) by these structures and some are actually amplified (reflected), much like a drum. The sound is then propelled out through our lips (some may escape through our nose as well) and out to the ears of the listener – but also to our own ears, which then respond by giving further instructions back to our brain. And all of this occurs within milliseconds of the idea being formed in our cortex.

'The whole process, and the end product of sound, voice, or speech, truly is "breath-taking". Much of it is out of our control (sub-conscious) but much is also within conscious control.

'There are so many systems at play simultaneously in the production of voice – much of the brain; the muscles of respiration, articulation and phonation; the laryngeal and peri-laryngeal muscles (strap muscles, tongue-base muscles and so on); the pharyngeal constrictors and muscles of swallow; the abdominal wall and thoracic wall

---

1 In adult males, the fundamental frequency of the conversational voice is approximately 80 to 130; in adult females, the fundamental frequency of the conversational voice is approximately 190–230.

muscles; and the deep postural muscles supporting the pelvis, thoracic and cervical spine – that many workers in the field feel that the entire body needs to be taken into consideration as the 'vocal organ'.

'The end product often seems and sounds effortless, and yet this is far from the case when the amount of energy required is considered. Not surprisingly, an almost inexhaustible amount of problems can impact on the production of voice and speech. These can start in the embryo, with imperfect formation of some of the structures (for example, cleft lip or palate, or incomplete or excessive fusion of the vocal cords), and continue right through life to those associated with the ageing process (for example, loss of elasticity of joints, thinning of the vocal ligaments, decreases in glands and glandular secretions).

'Problems as prevalent as the common cold, with post-viral cough, can prove very challenging, particularly for professional voice users, as they need to juggle issues relating to their health with their professional responsibilities. Allergy, postnasal drip, gastrointestinal and laryngo-pharyngeal reflux can all cause problems for the voice. Many systemic disorders can also worsen the voice. Thyroid issues have the potential to affect the vocal folds or the secretions produced on them; rheumatic disorders can affect the joints of the larynx. Stress-related disorders can make the voice worse. Most types of lung disorders, including asthma, chronic obstructive lung disease, emphysema and cancer, all have voice-related side effects – the list goes on.

'To help professional voice users with voice problems, the British Voice Association (the BVA) has supported the concept of multidisciplinary team-working in the form of voice clinics, for some twenty years. In the UK, there are now approximately one hundred voice clinics. The nucleus of each voice clinic is a highly specialised speech and language therapist (SLT) and an ENT surgeon with a special interest in laryngology. Some voice clinics also have direct access to other services, including physiotherapy or osteopathy, counselling or psychotherapy, gastroenterology and chest medicine.

'It is the recommendation of the BVA that anyone who is hoarse for more than two weeks would benefit from a review by an ENT surgeon. The typical route is through your GP. If your GP is concerned that the change in your voice might possibly be sinister, he or she will likely refer you to a "two-week wait" centre. More often, however, your GP will not be concerned by this possibility and will give a more general referral. They may have direct access to a voice clinic, or it may be that the ENT you see initially will then refer you on.

'When you are seen in the voice clinic, you can expect that the team will ask you to complete a questionnaire about your voice and how you feel about it, as well as take an unhurried and thorough history of your voice problem. As a part of the examination, they will examine your vocal folds directly, either with a nasendoscope (a small flexible tube) through your nose or with a rigid scope through your mouth. Both techniques will give a direct view of your vocal folds.

'Frequently, the team will use a technique called "stroboscopy" that will allow for an apparent slow-motion view of your vocal folds in action. Generally, they will play back this exam with you, and together with you will come up with a working diagnosis and treatment plan. This plan will frequently include vocal hygiene recommendations, such as drinking an adequate (not too much) amount of water, reducing caffeine intake, stopping nicotine products, as well as dietary and anti-reflux recommendations. They will likely either: reassure and discharge you back to your GP; refer you for focused speech therapy or other specialised services; or offer you laryngeal surgery with preoperative speech therapy.'

Roadie

In the early days, this is likely to be a friend or a relative who goes with you to your gigs or auditions and helps carry your equipment or just comes along for moral support. I've worked with a lovely singer whose dad was an incredibly famous footballer, who used to turn up at her gigs carrying her equipment. People used to do a double take every time they saw him.

You might prefer to go on your own, and that's fine, but if you don't have a manager at this stage, it's nice to have someone sitting in your dressing room with you or waiting in the queue of people outside the audition room, helping to make you feel less intimidated. Eventually, if you become a bit more successful, this role will become much more important and would be taken by a tour manager (see opposite).

Tour Manager

Ideally, your actual manager would be in the office working on all the paperwork side of your career and sorting out gigs and recording contracts for you. They wouldn't have time to go on tour with you or come to every gig, so this is where your tour manager would come in.

While you have to like and trust your manager, they're not necessarily someone who you'd call a mate. They'll come to some of your gigs, but you probably won't see them on a day-to-day basis. Your tour manager, on the other hand, is there for you twenty-four seven. He or she works for you, but also for your management, so they can report directly to them about all the business stuff you don't need to bother yourself with. But they also see to all the practicalities.

For instance, your tour manager will either be driving you themselves or organising a driver. They'll know at which hotel you're staying, what time the gig starts, where you go to next and so on. You'll rely on them a lot, and most artists have great relationships with their tour mangers, who stick with them for years.

A great example of a tour manager and artist relationship is Olly Murs and his tour manager, Mark Murphy. Every time I bump into Olly, Mark will also be there, a few steps behind. They're great mates, but Mark gets that work and friendship ratio just right.

Some people eventually employ a friend or relative to be their tour manager. If you have someone who'd be interested in doing that for you, they ought to look into it in a proper businesslike way. It can work really well, but only if strict rules and guidelines are set up from the start.

The *X Factor* runner-up from 2010, Rebecca Ferguson, employs her brother Sam as her PA. It works brilliantly for them. They have a great relationship, but they also know to give each other their individual space. Rebecca never takes advantage of Sam's time, and equally, Sam knows when Rebecca's opinion of something might differ from his. Just one more example of how important it is to have the right team of people behind you.

Paul Higgins started out working in security for Louis Walsh's bands Boyzone and Westlife in the nineties. In time, he became head of security and tour manager for, among others, Girls Aloud, Brian McFadden and Shayne Ward.

'Ultimately, I took on One Direction from the moment they came off *X Factor* in 2010 and worked with them for four years; forty of those forty-eight months were on the road, which was quite demanding as I have a very young family. The band are now on hiatus, so I've relaunched myself as a manager of a young Irish singer called Joe McVeigh, for whom I have high hopes.'

So what does a tour manager do? 'If you're taking on a young singer who's perhaps only sixteen or seventeen, it goes beyond a formal role and you become something that's a mix of father figure, chaperone and confidante. I'm also talking to their parents to let them know that I'm there to steady the ship when the youngsters are away from home, thrown into what is an alien and sometimes hostile environment.

'I'm there for their triumphs but also for their tears. I get to know every little thing about them. So it's very important that I really like whoever it is, because you're spending so much time with them. You get very, very close. As an example, Shayne is godfather to my first child.

'A tour manager works with the record label, the management company and the band. It's a crucial liaison role so it's a big responsibility. It helped that I had a background in security and that I'd travelled round the world so extensively from the beginning.

'But all of this has convinced me that I wouldn't want my own children to go into the music business. One minute, you're auditioning for a TV talent show; the next, you're catapulted into the spotlight and it can become very bewildering. It certainly makes you grow up fast. Look at Harry Styles and all he's been through. And he's still only twenty-three!

'My advice to anyone thinking of entering the industry? It's a great life, but try and be aware of what you're giving up to pursue your dream. You have to be mentally and physically strong for this job. The rewards can be fabulous. But they do come at a price.'

CHAPTER SEVENTEEN

IT'S A JUNGLE OUT THERE!

HOW TO SURVIVE IN THE MUSIC BUSINESS

Even if you are just starting out, it's good to have as much knowledge about the business you intend to go into as you can. It's one thing to do well in a TV talent show – even to win it – but quite another to build on that success and establish a lasting career. The music business is notoriously cut-throat and full of people with very short memories. So how, as a relative newcomer, do you make your mark, and who do you turn to in your bid to avoid becoming a one-hit wonder?

Well, you could do worse than consult my husband, Gordon Charlton. He began his career on a local newspaper, where he managed to review records as well as be a news reporter. He ended his journalistic career at the age of twenty as the pop writer on the *Daily Mirror*. Following this, he was offered a job as a talent scout by

CBS Records. He discovered Dead or Alive, Sade and the Pet Shop Boys, and when he became director of A&R, he signed Roachford, Deacon Blue and Bros. So there's not much he doesn't know about the business.

Says Gordon: 'Someone once said to me that you only ever become disillusioned if you had illusions in the first place. And I've never forgotten that. The most common illusion about the music industry is that you're going to become a star, remain a star and make lots of money. Well, you're not.'

But that didn't put him off. Eventually, he set up a pop label, Beautiful Noise, and signed Travis. For the last twenty years, he's worked as an independent manager and music publisher. 'And, in those two decades,' says Gordon, 'the industry has changed out of all recognition. When I started, album sales were the be-all and end-all. They were replaced in terms of importance by digital downloads, which more recently have faded away in favour of streaming income from the likes of Spotify and Apple Music.'

Streaming can be a big source of income. The Killers attracted 300 million streams for their single, 'Mr Brightside' on Spotify alone. At the time of writing the Spotify subscriber pays £10 a month and can then stream any music that's available on the streaming service. One million streams represent approximately £5,000 of income that Spotify will pay the owner of the recording. So, in this instance, that was £1.5m, which went straight to Universal Records, to whom the band are signed.

The charts these days have become much more volatile,

according to Gordon, because they include downloads, CDs *and* streams. Ten streams equals one sale.

An artist can generate money from streaming and downloads without the benefit of a record deal nowadays. They can fund the recording of an album through platforms like PledgeMusic or Kickstarter, and once the recordings are complete, they can sell the digital versions through a digital distributor such as AWAL, Believe or Ditto Music.

For all his informed cynicism, Gordon doesn't necessarily believe that wannabe singers should throw in the towel before they've tried to make their mark. He just wants to stress that you should set your sights on achievable targets: 'Then, if you work hard, it's possible to make a living for a lifetime. And just occasionally, one or two people get lucky. Jamie Lawson was in his late thirties, a jobbing musician making a living from playing gigs in small clubs. His publisher managed to get a track, "Wasn't Expecting That", released in Ireland. Ed Sheeran happened to hear it, tracked him down and signed him to his Gingerbread Man label. The record was a huge hit and won an Ivor Novello Award. The self-titled album that followed went to Number One. I think it's fair to say that Jamie wasn't expecting any of that! So it *can* happen.'

But you need to be savvy about possible sources of income: 'There are two sorts of rights holders when it comes to music: the people who own the recorded works and the people who own the actual compositions,' says Gordon. 'Every time a radio station plays a record, they have to pay the publisher of the song, which might, in this instance, be Jamie himself, or if he's sold the rights to a publisher, then they'd get the revenue.

'Digital income is weighted very heavily against the music publisher in favour of whoever owns the recording rights. It's why I always recommend to any of my artists that they retain the rights to their own material.'

He adds: 'I think the trick is to see yourself as a business, but the investment you make is not financial, it's your talent and the time you put into bringing that talent to as many people as possible. When I started doing A&R in 1982, there were so many fewer artists looking for record deals than there are today.

'Less than 1 per cent of people who think they're going to make it big in the business actually do so. Some people would say I'm being unnecessarily gloomy; I'd say I'm being realistic.'

Nick Fiveash qualified as a drama teacher, worked as a stagehand on West End shows for two years, became production manager on a string of pantomimes via which he got his Equity union card, and then moved into stage management. After a spell as a BBC floor and production manager, he gravitated towards the entertainment department, working on the likes of *Top of the Pops*, *Crackerjack*, *Victoria Wood*, *The Young Ones* and *The Late Late Breakfast Show*.

Recalls Nick: 'I'd just booked Terence Trent D'Arby on to *The Lenny Henry Show*, when his contact at CBS Records told me she was looking for someone to join the publicity team. She didn't have to ask twice. My first act was Alison Moyet, who I still look after thirty years later.

'In time, I also represented Barbra Streisand and Neil Diamond when they came to the UK. I got Mariah Carey on *Wogan*, her first ever TV in this country, and continued to work with her for ten years.'

In the mid-nineties, Nick (and a colleague) set up an independent PR company, taking some of those stellar names with him: 'Everyone was more interested in the pop acts, but I liked the artists with a proven pedigree.

'On my first day, I was offered the chance to work with Elaine Paige, and we're still together over twenty years later. I've worked extensively with Liza Minnelli and Charlotte Church, and I looked after the wonderful Cilla Black. My friends tease me that my agency – I now run it from a home office – ought to be called Divas R Us.'

So what's the point of a publicist? And are they really necessary? 'I know I would say this, but yes. I'm quite old-fashioned in the way I think publicity should be handled. I learnt that from Bobby Willis, Cilla Black's husband. He managed her career brilliantly.

'I'm a strong believer in not flooding the market with a particular artist. I prefer what I call "event PR". You do something when you've got something to promote. When you haven't, lie low. To my mind, a lot of publicity today is overkill. Turning up to the opening of an envelope means that the public is going to get bored of you.

'Alison Moyet is a great example of less is more. She'll keep her head down between projects, but then she'll pop up again and sell out three evenings in a row at the Albert Hall. She's never done eighties revival tours. She never gives interviews about her private life.

211

'She's always made a point of never chasing fame. You'll never see her on red carpets or turning up at premieres. Her attitude is: let the music speak for itself. And she's as popular three decades on as when she first launched. Her last album was Top Ten and her tours are always sold out.'

Clearly, it's a policy that has been shown to work. 'There's all the difference in the world,' says Nick, 'between a brief moment of fame, which is what can happen as a result of being on a talent show, and someone who wants a lifetime career. If I were handling someone who'd been on a talent show, I'd put them out on the road, not just via the *X Factor* tour, but thirty dates, say, when they could hone their craft and find their audience.

'You hear all this nonsense talked about an artist landing a ten million pound deal over ten years. But you've got to pay for the albums to be made, pay for the marketing, pay for the publicity, and then what happens when the third album's a flop? Suddenly, you're released from your record company deal.

'It's a tough business. Not so long ago, a young artist came to me who'd been on *X Factor*. She hadn't made the final ten and I had to be brutally honest with her. As I explained, even some of the people in the top five find it hard to sustain a career. You get break-out acts like One Direction and JLS, but they're the exceptions.

'And no matter how much massive Saturday night exposure you've had, people will quickly forget about you. I once worked with someone who came second, who had two Number One albums, but with the third, I couldn't get them arrested.'

What advice, then, would he give someone thinking of auditioning for a talent show? 'Be prepared – to give your absolute best, but also for rejection. And not just on the show but afterwards. Apart from the tens of thousands who audition, there's every chance that some of the final twelve who emerge will be back doing their day jobs very quickly.

'The way to buck the trend is to play pubs and clubs. There are lots of live gigs available these days, but you've got to be really passionate if you're going to make your mark. In the end, the question I would ask is: do you want to be an artist or do you want to be famous? Because there's a wealth of difference between the two.

'When I first started in the business, acts would expect to release at least a couple of albums before they had a hit single. Artists were allowed to grow; record companies would nurture them. Now, it's all about instant success. I worked with the band Deacon Blue, and they'd done something like a hundred and fifty gigs before they released an album and had a hit, and that's because they'd built up a huge fan base and were great at what they did.

'To my mind, there's no substitute for building up your core audience. And one of the best ways of testing your popularity is via social media. Even a long-established artist like Elaine Paige has a Twitter account. What a publicist like me can do is get you exposure on TV, radio and in the press that complements anything you might do yourself, along with a record release or tour.

'Talent shows are seen as a quick and easy route to stardom. But that very rarely happens. Someone can burn very brightly but very briefly. And the fall from grace can be very hard to take.

'But it's more than that. In my experience, it's harder to make it these days. I don't think we'll ever see again the likes of the massive superstars from the sixties and seventies – everyone from The Beatles to David Bowie and Elton John.

'For me, it stopped dead in the nineties when the accountants moved into the record industry. It was no longer being about artist growth and development, it was all about the bottom line. And none of them thought the Internet was a threat! I remember sitting in a meeting at CBS/Sony where a money man held up a CD and announced: "There'll never come a day when people won't want to own a physical copy of one of these."'

Rich Dawes is the managing director of PR company DawBell: 'I worked with Gary Barlow on X Factor for three consecutive years, so I saw the inner workings of a TV talent show at first hand.'

That makes Rich an ideal man to ask what a runner-up in a talent show should do once it's over. 'The first thing would be to find a manager as quickly as possible to capitalise on your TV profile, before people forget who you are. You need someone who can get you through the doors of PR companies and record labels as well as negotiate any potential deals with celebrity magazines.

'If there's too much attention, your manager should suggest you appoint a PR company – like ours – to help you navigate the choppy waters of the tabloid press. And make sure that your relationship with a manager, publicist, whoever, is collaborative. You may not have much experience, but don't agree to something if it doesn't feel right. As with everything in life, trust your instincts.

'It's also a smart idea while you're still on the show to make yourself known to the team, to build up a body of contacts, as well as picking up as many tips as possible from whoever is your mentor. Don't assume that because you've been on the show, you're set up for life.

'If you want proof of that, take the example of Rick Astley, who bounced back in 2016, aged fifty, with a Number One album, years after his original chart-topping success. If you can possibly pull a few strings and have a cup of tea with someone like that, you'd learn a huge amount. You'd certainly be struck by how grounded they are.

'If it were me looking to my future, I'd like to see a plan from my new manager as soon as possible on where they thought I'd fit as an artist in the business. In this day and age, you can't just put a record out on the basis that you've had a bit of airtime. What you need is a pre-determined strategy that includes the best producers and songwriters with whom you should work. And it's never a good idea to necessarily leave that decision to the record label.

'It's worth noting that as much as a talent show can shine the spotlight on you, it can also be a millstone. You don't just want to be defined by having once appeared on X *Factor*. That's no longer true of Leona Lewis or Olly Murs or One Direction. But they tend to be the exceptions. Who, though, remembers Steve Brookstein?

'From my company's point of view, the best bet is a new artist with a record deal, with music we like and with a manager we know and trust. That's immediately three ticks. But we do take on smaller acts without record deals although they tend not to come through reality TV shows; it would usually be through word of mouth.'

So what happens if you turn out to be one of the small percentage who do hit the big time? Rich Dawes cites a recent mental health awareness initiative, which made clear that unfamiliar success also has its downside.

Fiona McGugan, general manager of the Music Managers Forum, writing in the *Guardian* pointed out: 'Life in the music industry is likely to take its toll on a person regardless of mental vulnerability. Being thrust into the spotlight can be difficult enough – never mind the added pressures of completing a busy promo circuit or travelling the world on a non-stop tour – but it can also expose or create much deeper problems.

'In the music industry, there should arguably be no greater working relationship than that between an artist and their manager. Far from the cliché of a cigar-chomping penny counter, a good modern music manager will protect their client's emotional, mental and physical welfare just as passionately as their business interests. It's a role that can make all the difference for artists who may be struggling with the demands of stardom, along with any other mental health challenges.'

It's a view echoed by Marc Marot, a former UK record label boss and chairman of Crown Talent Management, which has the likes of Ella Henderson (*X Factor* favourite in 2012) and Jay McGuiness (The Wanted) on its books. 'If there's one thing that's for sure,' says Marot, 'it's that success and adulation never made any human being any more normal.

'What we're trying to do for our artists on a daily basis is make them more extraordinary. So we're setting people up to have a different way of thinking from the rest of humanity. Then we wonder why they think differently!'

One website, MusicSupport.org, appears to be a big step in the right direction. A non-profit collective providing confidential help and support for individuals across the UK music business, it's driven by industry figures like Chris Difford from Squeeze, tour manager Andy Franks and session musician Rachael Lander alongside clinical director Johan Sorensen.

Meanwhile, the Music Managers Forum (MMF) has been researching the potential for a range of resources to help young and established managers deal with mental illness and addiction – whether it's their clients who are affected or anyone else on the large teams many artists require to help handle success.

As MMF co-chair Diane Wagg explains: 'We looked at all the training we do for managers. The thing that seemed to be missing was that we weren't teaching our membership what to do when a client is having real problems – a nervous breakdown, relationship issues on tour, writers' block, panic attacks on stage.'

It's a subject close to the heart of singer Rumer – diagnosed with bipolar disorder and post-traumatic stress disorder – who feels that the biggest positive impact can come simply from putting small things in place to help look after an artist.

'The music industry needs to understand the physical, mental and emotional strain that acts are under,' she says. 'I remember thinking to myself, "I now know why people take drugs. They're not trying to kill themselves, they're trying to stay alive."'

And no one, it seems, is immune. Listen to Gary Barlow, arguably Britain's most successful singer-songwriter: '[Back in the nineties] I wasn't happy for a long period, and when you know what that feels like, then I don't care who you are, you're going to wake up some mornings and you're going to feel s***.

'You're going to have your winter days, and I know what that feeling's like and I hate it. I'll do anything to get me from that space. I'll go for a run, I'll have an ice bath, I'll watch my son's football game… I know what I need to do to get out of it. And that means I have to keep working.'

Gary says he's never met a major performer who wasn't vulnerable to the dread of depression: 'Because it's an indescribable thing, waving off at Hyde Park, and as far as the eye can see, there's hands waving back at you. Now, that's not normal. So in the balance of life, some time in the following week, it's got to go from the ceiling to the floor – it just has to.'

Jonathan Shalit is a British talent manager and chairman of ROAR Global and PR company Cole Kitchenn. He's clear-eyed, he says, when it comes to the entertainment industry: 'It's a business with no logic, no fairness, but with a huge amount of luck. That said, I've always believed that luck is where preparation meets opportunity.

'I would urge any young, aspiring, creative person to

keep on creating, no matter what. Associate with creative people. Go to places where creative people go. And never say never. Everybody is one phone call, one conversation away from potential success.

'Craig David had been a laughing stock for ten years. Then he made an amazing record and his career was back on track. It can happen to anyone, anywhere, any time. Julia Roberts had been knocked back over and over again. She was fourth choice to play *Pretty Woman* – and it changed her career. So my message is simple: if you believe, never give up.'

For five years, ROAR has had a contract with Simon Cowell and his company Syco to represent the winners of *Britain's Got Talent*. 'Last year, we also started working with eight of the finalists in *X Factor*, including the final three: Matt Terry, Saara Aalto and 5 After Midnight. All of them have the prospect of long and successful careers. All of them, in my opinion, will still be performing five years from now.'

From his roster of talent, who can Shalit give as an example of someone whose career he nurtured and built to the point where they remain a potent force?

'Myleene Klass,' he says. 'She was one of the winners of *Popstars*, the first talent show of recent times, becoming one of the members of Hear'Say.

'Now, fourteen years later, she's still at the top of her game. Quite apart from her naturally warm personality, Myleene has a terrific work ethic and an ability to connect with people. Yes, she also has musical talent – she's a classically trained pianist with a beautiful singing voice – but she wouldn't have been as successful as she has been if she had a personality that got on people's nerves. Emma Bunton is hugely likeable, too. So are Lorraine Kelly and Katherine Jenkins and boxer Nicola Adams, all of whom we represent.'

So what about the also-rans? How do they capitalise on their brief moment of fame?

'I say the same thing to all of them. Keep performing. Keep writing. Keep evolving. And remember: sometimes you don't have to be the best.

'Take Jedward. I think even they might acknowledge they weren't abundantly talented, musically speaking, but they have masses of personality and have gone on to make a lot of money by exploiting that. They even represented Ireland twice in Eurovision.'

And while there may be more competition than ever, there are also more opportunities, insists Jonathan. 'We're in a golden age of entertainment, I really believe that. If you look at the charts, at television, at cinema, there's a huge resource of talent out there and a huge number of outlets for it. Look at the multiplicity of channels available, for instance. It's very exciting.

'So more choice, but more competition too. And that's healthy. It certainly benefits the consumer, but it also benefits the individual performer because it means you raise your game.

'And never say never. If you're short, fat and ugly but have your heart set on becoming a movie star, go for it. None of those things held back Danny DeVito. In the end, you've got to believe in yourself more than anybody else does – apart from your mum.'

CHAPTER EIGHTEEN

SINGING IS GOOD FOR YOU!

WHY YOU DON'T HAVE TO WIN A TALENT CONTEST TO ENJOY HITTING THE HIGH NOTES

Not everybody wants to have a career in singing, of course. A lot of people are very happy for it to be their hobby, and there's absolutely no reason why you shouldn't learn to sing to the best of your ability for the sheer sense of achievement and the enjoyment it will bring. For example, singing in a choir or with a group of people can be truly beneficial.

As a child, I was always in choirs, and it became a way of life for me. It's also a very useful discipline for the young. You're learning words and music in a classroom. Or you're accepting the responsibility of turning up at the right place at the right time and doing what the teacher or choir leader is telling you. But on top of all that, it can and should be good fun.

My only sadness is that more and more children – especially at secondary school in the state sector – are offered less and less chance to sing. I know from experience that children who are really shy can start off at the back of the choir, but gradually, they gain the confidence to come nearer to the front and not hide at the back. It's almost as if they forget to be nervous.

I liked singing so much that I sang in a local choral society from about the age of seven and then all through my childhood. It was a great way of making new friends and joining in a group activity. I loved being part of the sound a choir makes together – it's exhilarating, exciting. I'll never forget the time we sang with an orchestra in a large theatre in Aberdeen in front of hundreds of people. I felt so proud of myself; we all did.

On one occasion – I must have been ten by then – we were chosen to sing a new version of 'All Things Bright and Beautiful' on BBC1's *Songs of Praise*. Obviously, it was important that we all sang in tune, but the choirmaster came up with a neat solution. He told us that if we were even a little unsure of certain passages, not to risk it and just to mime those words. He could have thrown out any dodgy singers, but he was kind enough and astute enough to know that this was a big deal for all of us. It would have been a bitter blow to be asked to stand down before our big TV performance.

In my next choir, there was an incredible choirmaster called Donald Hawksworth who taught us a lot. One of his exercises was to make us sing a tongue twister – 'Popocatepetl, copper-plated kettle' – over and over, which I still use as a warm-up before a performance. (Popocatepetl is an active volcano in Mexico.)

Later on, when I was a student at the Royal Scottish Academy of Music and Drama, we had the principal, Sir Philip Ledger, conducting our choir. It was deadly serious. He loved scaring us and we were suitably terrified. The fear factor wouldn't necessarily be my chosen method of teaching, but wow, we learnt so much from him! And because I wanted singing to be my career, I was striving to be the best I possibly could. We sang Verdi's *Requiem* at the City Hall in Glasgow – I'll never forget it, it was stunning.

If you want to be a soloist in later life, there's no substitute for the grounding you receive in your formative years from singing with a choir. It taught me about breathing, vocal flexibility, dealing with runs, how to fit in the words, and how to read music: it was invaluable. It certainly gave me the confidence to become a performer when eventually I left school.

My life has now gone full circle, because I'm quite often invited to judge choirs in competitions – sometimes in schools, sometimes on television. For instance, back in 2008, I was involved as the vocal coach in a BBC1 series called *Last Choir Standing*. What struck me at the time was the diversity. There was a young gospel choir, a choir made up of older people, a male voice choir and so on. But they were all on the same journey: learning to sing as one, learning to put across their particular story.

Despite the good work done by Gareth Malone (*The Choir*), I still think a lot of people don't realise the extent of choral societies up and down the UK. When I was a young professional singer, much of my work would be as a featured soloist with these choirs. I learnt my trade performing as a soloist with choral societies in towns up and down the country, and eventually was booked for larger and more prestigious venues such as the Queen Elizabeth Hall and the Royal Festival Hall. It became my musical education throughout my twenties.

It's a myth to imagine that local choirs are made up exclusively of little old ladies. I encountered a wide mix of generations, with a real sense of this being a social event. But no matter your age, it's clear to me that singing is good for you. When you sing, you release endorphins, as you do when you exercise, so you always feel better when you've finished, and not least because you've also released emotions, both happy and sad, which is so much better than bottling them up.

This is true whether you're a child, someone suffering from a neurological condition like Parkinson's or dementia, or dealing with emotional issues like loneliness. Singing is good for the soul!

This is a sentiment heartily endorsed by Leonora Davies MBE, who's been involved with music since 1965 as a teacher, co-ordinator and head of department in primary and secondary schools, before becoming inspector for music in the London Borough of Haringey. She now works as a freelance music education consultant, which includes being a mentor for regional and national festivals for Music for Youth, a British charity which provides free access to educational and performance opportunities for groups of young musicians and audiences throughout the UK.

'I come from a musical family and always sang at school,' says Leonora. 'To this day, I can remember singing the soprano solo on "I Know That My Redeemer Liveth" from *The Messiah* with the school choir.' When she completed her subsequent course at Bretton Hall, a music and art college in Yorkshire, she began her career as a class music teacher.

'My ambition was to encourage children to sing and play instruments together, and it had, as it always does, the most extraordinarily transformative effect. No child will fully understand the joy of music unless they're immersed in it. And the element that's appealing to me is that everyone can do it because we've all got a voice.

'Everyone can smile. Everyone can open and close their eyes. And, to a greater or lesser extent, everyone can sing. I often say when I'm mentoring a choral session that I like to see a choir singing with their eyes.'

Leonora will never forget the five years she spent teaching in Tower Hamlets in east London. Over 90 per cent of the children were Bangladeshi, so English wasn't even their first language: 'I remember a class of six- and seven-year-olds, such shy little things. They started by looking down at the floor the whole time, until that magical moment when, as part of a circle game, I'd see more and more beautiful big eyes looking up at me, and if I was lucky, accompanied by a smile. Proof, if it were needed, that music crosses every known barrier.'

Music is also a wonderful way, she says, of teaching

language: 'Melody and rhythm help children remember vocabulary. But singing is also physiologically very good for you. It's to do with your breathing and posture, and your brain, with remembering a tune and some words. The fact that it also comes from inside yourself, of course, is part and parcel of building self-confidence. Suddenly being able to produce a note, even if it isn't always quite in tune, is very good for a child's self-esteem.

'Getting young children to participate in whole class singing is never wasted energy. But it's very important that no child should be made to feel that they're standing out. Young children can often be reluctant to sing because they might be shy and lacking in self-confidence. So I always encouraged them to do a number of simple exercises before we started singing – like rolling their shoulders, clapping their hands, closing and opening their eyes and finally giving me a big smile. Children can arrive in class feeling grumpy for whatever reason. But involving them in a group activity that's fun will inevitably change their mood. There's no doubt that singing is an enormously joyful and bonding experience.'

This is why Leonora is such a big fan of Sing Up. An award-winning initiative, Sing Up was launched in 2007 to provide a complete singing package for schools through resources, training and guidance, with the aim of deepening children's understanding of music and singing, raising attainment and developing lasting tools for children to express themselves with confidence and creativity.

Directed at primary school children, government funding for Sing Up came to an end after three years, although many individual schools and the music publishing company, Faber, have continued to support the scheme. For more details, visit *www.singup.org*

Says Leonora: 'I received any number of letters from head teachers saying that singing as a class and as a whole school activity had transformed their schools. That didn't come as a surprise to me. Introduce singing into the curriculum, and children start to feel confident about something that isn't academic in the strict definition of that word. Even now, the teaching of music in state schools is still statutory up to the end of Year Nine – that is, for children up to the age of fourteen. It becomes a lot more hit-and-miss beyond then.

'That's a sadness to me because I know from experience that the beneficial effects of singing on young people in their formative years is immeasurable.'

Professional soprano Nicola Wydenbach knows a lot about the restorative physical effects of singing on people with Parkinson's. Her late father-in-law had it, and she now works regularly with Parkinson's groups: 'One in five hundred people are living with the condition,' says Nicola, 'and that number rises to one in a hundred for the over-sixties.

'Although we think of shaking as the main symptom, there are many different manifestations of Parkinson's, including the weakening of the voice. One day, I was round at my father-in-law's house when he was having a speech therapy session. I noticed that many of the exercises were comparable to how I warmed up as a singer.'

A quick Google search revealed that Nicola's hunch

was correct: singing could take over from where speech therapy left off. The mechanical processes of singing can help support physical functions in people with Parkinson's, including exercises to promote facial, throat and chest muscle mobility as well as vocal clarity and strength. Moreover, deep breathing encourages improved lung capacity while postural exercises assist standing stability and walking pace.

Nicola was determined to learn more. In 2014, she won a scholarship from the Finzi Trust to visit the Tremble Clefs, a pioneering organisation in California which had extended speech therapy exercises for people with Parkinson's through group singing.

Back in the UK, she hooked up with Professor Grenville Hancox, whose Canterbury and Pimlico Skylarks were working in the same field as part of his Canterbury Cantata Trust. 'All these encounters convinced me that there needed to be training for potential leaders to run singing groups for people with the condition,' says Nicola.

For the past two years, as part of an ongoing Aldeburgh residency at the Maltings in Suffolk, Nicola has been running courses for people wanting to set up their own groups all over the UK, Ireland and even Australia. She's now taken over Grenville's Pimlico group while running another in Chatham, Kent, and more recently yet another at King's College Hospital in Denmark Hill, London.

'But most excitingly of all,' she says, 'Grenville and I are now in the process of launching a national umbrella organisation, Sing to Beat Parkinson's. Our ultimate goal is for every one of the three hundred and sixty-five or so branches of Parkinson's UK to have its own locally-run singing group.'

As Nicola points out, speech therapy, while useful, is usually a solitary experience; it is expensive, and it isn't fun. By contrast, group singing can lift the spirits and take you out of yourself. 'The social aspect is pretty important, too; no one has any inhibitions about their condition, for the simple reason that everyone, to a greater or lesser extent, is in the same boat.'

She has countless examples of witnessing at first hand the beneficial effects of singing on people with Parkinson's: 'As good as any is a chap called Tony, who's probably now in his seventies and whose condition is clear to anyone who meets him. When he speaks, you can hardly hear a word he's saying because his voice is so thin and weak.

'We did a concert when the Pimlico Skylarks joined their Canterbury equivalents and Tony sang a solo. You could hear every word. I knew how singing had strengthened his voice over the weeks and months, but that didn't stop me sobbing my heart out. He normally uses a walking frame, but because of the adrenaline induced by the whole experience, he didn't need it for the rest of the day.

'People with Parkinson's often suffer from what is called a frozen gait. They'll find it difficult on occasion to keep moving. It's been shown that the release of endorphins when you sing will reactivate the body. So it's not only the vocal muscles that benefit, but people's mobility too. What's more, group singing appears to have more benefit than singing on your own.'

Glenn Bassett enthusiastically echoes Nicola's words.

And he knows what he's talking about. He calculates that he must now have led about 750 Singing for the Brain sessions for the Alzheimer's Society, and about the same number at local day centres for people with learning difficulties and dementia and their carers.

After working with the homeless in his early twenties, he got a job providing support work in the community for people with various mental health problems: 'There was a drumming group in my local area in north London for people with learning difficulties, so I volunteered my services. I also joined a band as a rhythm guitarist, although I prefer to think of myself as a strummer rather than a musician.'

In time, he became known as someone who, at short notice, could stand in at a gathering of people with dementia and entertain those present with a few songs. He first became aware of Singing for the Brain in 2010, and slowly, it took over his working life.

'In terms of how to lead a session, it's a matter of taste. Some leaders like the sessions to be mostly a series of therapeutic musical exercises and games. Although I do include some of those exercises, personally I like to focus more on having a good old singalong and a dance. To my way of thinking, such sessions can be every bit as therapeutic as something more formal.

'I try to create an atmosphere in the room where everyone feels they're having a party, because that feeling will stay with them and also make them want to return. I'm not performing for them; I'm leading them in singing songs, which is why I deliberately join everyone by sitting with them in a circle. We have half an hour at the beginning for tea and coffee and welcoming everybody, followed by an hour of music, before ending up with another half hour of chat.

'Social gatherings for people with dementia can often be quite stressful. If you can't remember somebody's name or what's just been said, you tend to retreat into your shell. It's striking that once those same people come into the circle and start singing, all their inhibitions seem to fall away. Everyone's equal; you're in the moment with the songs.'

It's extraordinary, says Glenn, how people can sing all the verses to a song they first learnt fifty or sixty years ago. According to the late British neurologist, Oliver Sacks: 'Music evokes emotion and emotion brings with it memory. It brings back the feeling of life when nothing else can.'

The Alzheimer's Foundation of America sums it up like this: 'When used appropriately, music can shift mood, manage stress-induced agitation, stimulate positive interactions and coordinate motor movements. This is because music requires little to no mental processing, so singing doesn't involve the cognitive function absent in most dementia patients.'

And the effects last for longer than the session: 'I like to quote one man,' says Glenn, 'who told me: "For two days after a Singing for the Brain session, my wife says I'm bearable again."'

So what are the sure-fire winners that get everyone in the group joining in?

'I often start with "Singin' in the Rain" because it sounds like Singing for the Brain; then it might be a bit of rock'n'roll in the middle – everything from Buddy Holly to "Blue Suede Shoes" – then something from The Beatles, like "All You Need Is Love" or "With a Little Help from My Friends", then Abba's "Waterloo". What I'm aiming for is participation, which is why I always like to end with something simple that everyone can join in with, like "Show Me the Way to Go Home".'

It's not hard to see what the people with dementia and Alzheimer's get out of Glenn's singing sessions. But what about him?

'I always quote something a colleague said to me a couple of years ago when she attended a Singing for the Brain session in Redbridge.

'At the end, she said: "I just want to say to everybody that I have been with the Alzheimer's Society for twenty-two years and this is the most fun I've ever had." And I thought to myself: "Yes, and I get to do this five times a week."

'I never want to stop. Why would I retire? In fact, if I won the lottery tomorrow, I'd carry on doing exactly what I'm doing right now.'

Whether you want to perform at local gigs, join a choir or be the next *X Factor* winner, singing has something for everyone.

It's never too late to start.

It makes you feel alive, and as we have seen in this chapter, can be so beneficial for both your mental and physical health.

Don't put it off – just give it a go!

CHAPTER NINETEEN

FREQUENTLY ASKED QUESTIONS

Earlier in this book we briefly discussed questions that I am constantly asked, and I was explaining that yes, having secure vocal technique will help with most things. Let's go into detail now on how we fix these common problems. When members of the public come up and randomly ask me about singing, the number one question without a doubt is...

1. Can you teach anyone to sing?

The answer to that is, if someone is tone-deaf, then I can't really, because if they can't even hear the notes they are trying to sing, or if they can't hear that they are 'way out', there isn't much hope! However, some people say to me, 'I'm tone-deaf,' and when I hear them, they are fine. So if you really want to sing and you think this is your problem, ask someone if you are in tune.

We all know when we hear people singing out of tune – we all shout at our TV screens when we hear them or collectively groan on Twitter. Sometimes being out of tune isn't to do with a problem with your musical ear, it's caused instead by not using the muscles properly or something as simple as the sound set-up being totally wrong at your gig.

If you aren't tone-deaf but have a problem with tuning, it's something you need to discuss with a singing teacher to see what is causing it. It's not something I can fix here because it depends on whether you are flat or sharp (under or above the note). If you really are tone-deaf, have fun singing, but I don't think it's your best career option.

2. I always feel really awkward walking into an audition. It's as though suddenly I can't even walk properly. What's the best way to enter an audition? Should I be confident, or will that annoy the panel?

Here are the options:

(a) You fling the door open, bound into the room, shake everyone's hand and announce yourself.

(b) You slowly enter the room, smiling politely, and wait until you are spoken to.

(c) You act as if you are extremely honoured to be there and make a big deal of looking humble and nervous. You want the panel to think you are a lovely, down-to-earth person, not at all cocky, and want to surprise them with how good you are, when you are obviously unaware of it yourself.

(d) You walk confidently into the room and say, 'Hello, I'm John Smith, nice to meet you all.'

(e) You are so scared, you don't even know what you are doing body-language wise.

So which one is correct? That's the problem: there isn't a right or wrong way because every single one of those people could get the part, but some are making things difficult for themselves before they even begin.

Personally, I can see through the bull****. If people pretend to be humble but are not, it just comes over as an act. It might work on TV, but unless your acting is Oscar standard, don't bother in the audition room. If people bound over to me and I'm in the mood for that, brilliant, but how do you know what mood we are all in? So don't be overly friendly and try too hard.

Here's a little audition panel secret: we usually have hand sanitiser under the desk because we have to shake hands with hundreds of people. The worst type are the ones who enthusiastically shake our hands then tell us the story of how ill they have been for the last twenty-four hours and that they hope their voice will come out.

Inside I'm silently screaming, 'Keep your germs to yourself!'

OK, I'm a bit OCD, so I'm probably not the best person to shake hands with, but I'm not alone – there must be other people like me. It's enough to say hello or thank you.

For me, hand shaking isn't a must, but don't worry, I have put through many people who have given me a handshake and I don't hold it against them! Of course I'm just talking personally. Many people on panels will offer you their hands to shake as soon as you come in. Simply gauge it on the day. If you come into an audition and it's me there, just give me a wave!

Now I've digressed from the actual walking, so let's talk about that.

Posture is important for any performer, so coming in like a performer is important. Here, I want to immediately see you look like a singer and have the posture of a singer. If you are going to wear heels in the audition, practise wearing them. I have some fabulous heels that look great while I'm standing still or sitting, or even walking a few paces, but if I have to do a long walk across a room with everyone looking at me, I will choose another pair. If the heels are too unstable or a little bit too high so that walking is awkward, choose a slightly less towering pair perhaps or a chunkier, more stable heel. But always practise with them on; heels can dramatically change your posture and therefore your singing.

Now let's assume this isn't an audition, it is a gig, and it's somewhere you'll have a long walk to your position. Again, practise in the shoes you will be wearing. We don't want to see that bent-knees strut so often seen on the high street on a Saturday night; we prefer an assured, 'Look at me, I could walk in these for hours.' Most of the time you boys won't have a heel problem, but still, practise your walk and make sure you are comfy and look and feel at ease.

3. No matter what I do, I can't shake off my nerves and it's ruining my performances. What can I do?

Nerves are SO annoying! No matter who you are or what level you're at, they can suddenly strike. Personally, I find the smaller and more intimate the gig or audition, the greater my nerves. When singing to a large crowd, I seem to be able to get into the zone, but when people are near me and I can see the whites of their eyes, the palpitations start.

To those of you who haven't experienced proper nerves, you are lucky and maybe you won't. However, if it happens at some gig in the future, just try to keep breathing. First of all, your heart starts beating out of your chest and you find that it's hard to actually breathe properly. Then you will suddenly get the leg shake. If you haven't experienced it before, it comes as a bit of a shock: you will try to stop your leg from shaking, but it just won't. You assume everyone can see it and that it looks ridiculous, but they are almost certainly totally oblivious to it. Now, assuming that you have worked on your diaphragmatic breathing, as we discussed in Chapter Six, just concentrate on that. Thankfully, you are not singing with your leg, and so long as you can control your voice, your leg will look after itself. Shifting your weight or just taking a couple of steps can help, but your leg probably won't stop shaking now until you come off stage, so just try to ignore it. At this point you will be glad if your shoes are not too wobbly and the heels are not too high.

At the same time as your leg starts to shake, your mouth goes incredibly dry. This is not a normal dryness, but an overwhelming dryness where your tongue glues itself to the roof of your mouth. (Pineapple juice does seem to help with this dryness, so give it a try.) The only way to stop this happening is to perform or audition as often as you can. Your body gets used to the amount of adrenaline you experience when you perform, and realises that you are not in a life-threatening situation but a situation you have chosen to be in as your job (you must be crazy!).

Believe it or not, you will get used to this adrenaline rush. You will be able to control your nerves much better over time. Occasionally though, your nerves will just appear when you are least expecting them, and like me, you will probably find that it's at a smaller gig you shouldn't even be scared of.

Many of my singers who are performing on live TV or at huge stadium gigs or festivals experience dreadful nerves because of the enormity of the situation. However, I've had singers who have performed at the Oscars, the Grammys, presidential inaugurations and all the huge American TV chat shows, but they are more nervous before a small interview or an intimate gig.

Nerves are part of life for all performers. Some find it so hard, they turn to alcohol or drugs, and of course there are so many stories of high-profile performers who have to 'use' something to help. The sad thing is that it never helps, so seek professional advice for your nerves rather than thinking you can self-medicate. Brilliant breath control, hypnotherapy, mindfulness, counselling or simply learning to believe in yourself are the only things which I have seen work. Also, as we have discussed before, the more you prepare, the less likelihood there is of anything going wrong; after all, that's really the only thing we are worrying about, isn't it?

I always have a pact with my singers: I promise to do the worrying and all they have to do is sing. You may say that isn't going to work, but it actually does. If you build up total trust in your vocal coach and believe they will help you with all your worries, it takes a huge weight off your mind. When you're not afraid to break down in front of them or have them see you at your most vulnerable, and if you know they will always tell you the truth about how well or badly you sing, you will actually feel that a problem shared is a problem halved. No longer is anything your problem, for you to lie awake and worry about, it's a shared problem. You can then discuss it and hopefully sort it out before you go on stage and start panicking about it.

It's easier if you are in a band because hopefully you have the back-up of the others, but as a solo artist, you have a lot to deal with alone. So lean on your coach – good vocal coaches know all about their singers' psyches. Remember, you don't have to be alone: help is at hand and you just have to ask for it.

4. I always get a bit hoarse by the end of my gigs; how can I increase my stamina?

It's a lot more common than you think to have this problem, honestly. Many singers come to me with the same worry, and nine times out of ten it is caused by singing from your throat and not using the rest of your body, including your diaphragm, to help.

If we took a video of you performing, we would probably see the tension in your throat or neck. We would also probably see you tensing up more and more as you got tired. Then, as you could feel your voice wasn't responding, we would see and hear you pushing your voice harder and harder in order to get to your notes. The result? A sore throat, a hoarse sound and even permanent damage to your voice.

I hear you saying you have tried to do the correct breathing, you have tried to sing properly, but it isn't working. Have you actually practised, or are you just too tired after gigs to sing during the day? Is it a vicious cycle: when you sound bad, you try too hard to sound better and end up sounding worse?

STOP, just completely STOP.

Checklist

- Take a day to rehearse your set list. First, make sure you have had lots to drink, and then warm up your voice slowly.
- Now look in the mirror: look at the way you are holding your microphone and study your posture. Refer to pages 59-62 if you can't remember how it should be.
- Now sing any song you are unhappy with to 'vvvvv', using your diaphragm (see also page 66). Feel the flow of your breath. Now sing it to the words.

- Go through each song and keep checking that everything is correct. Hopefully you will notice when you are doing something that is causing the problem. It might be jaw tension, shoulder tension, pulling too much weight in your voice up to the top (remember, we sometimes need brighter vowels on the way up, as the notes before the high ones can be the problem). Just go back to previous chapters and re-read.

- Maybe your songs are in too high a key (you might need to think about finding a lower version or another song). In my experience, instead of panicking, being proactive and practising your technique always helps. If you are doing things correctly, your stamina will improve. It's just about ticking off the checklist of things that could be standing in your way. So don't beat yourself up.

  If you have been singing three songs before getting tired, congratulate yourself when, at your next gig, you sing four before that happens.

  Give yourself a break. Remember, you are mastering this singing lark and it just takes time. Don't forget, of course, to look back at Chapter Three, The Singer's Rulebook (pages 19–33).

  Pamper that voice of yours!

5. How do I get rid of the really obvious breaks in my voice? Sometimes I want to sing a big high note but a breathy little falsetto comes out instead.

This question comes up all the time. We obviously talked about this in detail in Chapter Seven, Let's Get Singing (pages 89–107), so I suggest you study that chapter again. However, here is a summing up of the 'breaks' problem.

- If an untrained singer sings up a scale, the voice will change at certain moments. We call these breaks gear changes or different registers. Even people who know nothing about singing can hear them – it's when a big gutsy sound suddenly becomes weedy and breathy.
- Some singers make that sound on purpose and it adds to their individuality. Think Dido, who flips in and out of falsetto all the time.
- Practising downwards scales to 'vvvvv' can help 'blend' those registers. Or you can go upwards as well, but try to keep the tone the same.
- Using the straw exercises we talked about earlier in Chapter Seven (page 94), which help you to have a higher placement, can help too.
- Gliding up and down scales to 'ng' (see also page 81) helps to exercise the muscles as you go across the breaks.
- As I have said before, I work with my singers to achieve one voice. We do this through all of the above and also working on one note at a time to perfect our vowels. I use the Italian term *passaggio*, which

describes the transitional area between breaks, in other words, a passageway. Don't think of sudden breaks, but rather an area in between, where you can mix the two sounds together and not have such a clunky sudden change of sound.

- With practice you can achieve this, and if you want that flip sound for specific songs, you can use it when you want it rather than having to use it because you have no idea how not to.

- I suggest you don't use that 'break' word anymore. I don't talk much about chest voice, head voice, falsetto and breaks. Instead, think about one voice linked by passageways when you go up and down. It takes time, but as well as excellent breathing, this is one of the techniques that will benefit you the most.

6. I'm so confused about what key to sing in. If I can hit the high notes at the end of some songs, the beginning is far too low, and if I put it in a higher key so I can sing the beginning, I can't reach the notes at the end. Help!

Many pop songs are written like this so that the chorus can sound dramatic. They start really low, and then when they get to the chorus, they either go up an octave or at least get quite a bit higher.

Let me tell you that even many of the singers who have recorded those songs have trouble with this. In recording studios, the producer often encourages the singer to sing at their absolute highest to achieve a really exciting version of the song. Who can blame them? They want it to be a hit. Besides, that feeling that the singer is giving his or her all is exciting in itself.

Here is the problem, though. If it's a hit, the singer has to perform that song over and over again, often at the end of a tiring gig. It's possible to lower a track by a semi-tone pretty quickly, and I remember asking a sound engineer to lower a song for a singer who was about to sing at a huge event live on TV. I've done this many times, but maybe not had it delivered with just five minutes to spare before the show! She was so happy though and sounded great.

Sometimes, when singers are really warmed up, the top notes are fine but the low notes at the beginning are a struggle. So let's assume you can get to the high notes and you are in a key where they are exciting but achievable. So how on earth do you get those low notes at the beginning of the song to sound good as well?

Let's use 'Run' by Gary Lightbody of Snow Patrol as an example. This was a really emotional song for Gary to write, and the beginning needs to be dark and meaningful. The melody is low in the voice at the start. Leona Lewis's version is the same – it's so low in her voice, but it has to have that dark, sad sound. I've worked with both Gary and Leona on this song, and here is the solution: we need to be sad, emotional and dark while still having enough resonance to keep in tune and be able to hear those low notes.

- The secret to getting low notes is not to darken your voice and go down to them, it's the opposite. You have to brighten the sound by not thinking of them as low at all. Yes, I know this sounds crazy, but you have to smile.

- Now I'm not talking about a grin showing your teeth. Remember in Chapter Seven we discussed the lines above and below which we 'do all the work'? I'm talking about the thing I call a 'singer's smile'. This is achieved by slightly lifting your cheekbones and thinking of the roof of your mouth as being like a dome shape – you can still look sad, but you will have a brightness that lifts the sound. This keeps dull low notes in tune and gives them a resonance.

- I get my singers to practise the melody to a witchy 'nya' sound until they feel how bright it needs to be, and then they can sing it to the words while feeling like they are still singing 'nya nya'. You will be surprised to learn that although you think by darkening the sound you will make the low notes easier, you will find it so much easier now you have brightened the sound. When Leona Lewis and I first worked on this version for Radio 1's *Live Lounge*, it was pretty amazing right from the start, and there was no question that the high notes were going to be spectacular and make it such a hit. The low notes therefore just had to be worked on to make them doable in that key. The result was incredible!

- We have discussed how to make a song your own, and Leona's version of 'Run' is like a masterclass in how to do this. So much so that I remember Gary Lightbody once saying at a Snow Patrol gig that year, 'We are now going to perform "Run" by Leona Lewis.' Whether I hear Snow Patrol or Leona's version of this song when I switch on the radio or walk into a show, I always have a tear in my eye. Gary Lightbody is a wonderful songwriter and such a lovely man.

There are dozens of questions like these, and hopefully most of them have been answered somewhere in this book, if not in this chapter. Many of the solutions to one problem can be similar to the solutions for others. Usually, if you build up a good technique by going back to basics and working through each technical stage slowly and carefully, you will be able to answer many of those questions yourself.

CHAPTER TWENTY

THE LANGUAGE OF MUSIC

(A GLOSSARY OF ALL THE WORDS YOU'LL NEED TO UNDERSTAND)

All dictionary definitions can be found in the *Collins English Dictionary*.

Arpeggio

'A chord whose notes are played in rapid succession rather than simultaneously.'
In singing, these are vocal exercises on sounds such as 'doh, me, soh, doh'.

Aspirate

To articulate an audible expulsion of breath. Examples would be the 'h' in how and happy.

Break

We all know that a break, such as a break in a plate, is where there's a crack down the middle, but a break in your voice is when your voice changes from one sound to another. It can actually sound like it's breaking or cracking when this gear change occurs and you're going from one vocal register to another. With training, this obvious 'break' can be smoothed out and the transition between registers made easier to deal with.

Diaphragm

'The diaphragm is a dome-shaped muscular partition that separates the abdominal and thoracic cavities in mammals.' When it contracts, the volume of the thorax is increased and this inflates the lungs. It therefore plays a major role in breathing.

Dynamics

In music, when we talk about the dynamics, we mean how loud or soft a sound might be – that is, the dynamic levels from *pianissimo* (the Italian term for 'very soft') to *fortissimo*, which means 'very loud'.

Edge

When we talk about 'edge' in relation to the voice, we're talking about a harder, more projected tone that cuts through, rather than a soft, pretty tone.

Falsetto

The breathy high sound achieved when the ligamentous edges (underneath edges) of the vocal folds vibrate while leaving the main body of each fold relatively relaxed.

Glottal

'Of or relating to the glottis'

The glottis is 'the vocal apparatus of the larynx, consisting of the two true vocal cords and the opening between them'. The glottal stop is 'a plosive speech sound produced as the sudden onset of a vowel in several languages ... by first tightly closing the glottis and then allowing the air pressure to build up in the trachea before opening the glottis, causing the air to escape with force'.

How to make a glottal stop: if you're unsure what all this means, imagine you're about to say: 'No, don't do that!' to a small child or even your cat or dog. The sound 'uh oh' will come out, and that's a glottal stop.

Head Voice

Head voice can often be described as feeling the vibrations of resonance in the head, however what this actually means is the vocal register where low diaphragmatic breathing, and thus a low larynx position, assists the fine edges of the vocal folds to vibrate at a higher frequency (pitch) producing an effortless tone.

Interval

An interval is the difference in pitch between two musical notes.

Key

Music is written in different scales or groups of notes. The key refers to the group of pitches in which a song or a piece of music is written or sung.

Larynx

A cartilaginous and muscular hollow organ forming part of the air passage to the lungs: in higher vertebrates it contains the vocal cords.

Legato

In music, many Italian terms are used. It's good to know the most popular of these. *Legato* means smooth, and refers to making a connected sound between notes, resulting in smooth-flowing musical phrases.

Musicality

This has got nothing to do with musical theatre. If you sing with musicality, it doesn't mean you'll sound like you're singing in a musical, as some people mistakenly think. It just means that you sing with a sensitivity of phrasing and have a natural feel for the music.

Although some people can be encouraged to play or sing with more musicality, quite often it's something that people are just born with a feeling for.

Passaggio

This is an Italian term used to describe the transitional area between vocal registers. Its literal meaning is passageway – it is good to imagine a passageway linking registers.

Range

The amount, number or type of something between an upper and lower limit. In singing, this means the notes you sing and where they are. Some singers have high ranges and others low; some have many notes in their ranges, others may be limited to a few. Your range is how low and how high you can sing comfortably and pleasantly.

Register

Within a singer's range there are several registers. These registers are areas of different resonances and tones produced by particular vibratory patterns of the vocal folds.

Resonance

The quality in a sound of being deep, full and reverberating: for example, think of when you go into a cave and shout. Your voice reverberates and sounds very resonant.

Riff

A riff is a short, repeated phrase in popular music and jazz, typically used as an introduction or refrain in a song. In singing, a riff is a set of notes that quite often shows off the vocal range or just the flexibility of the voice. It's also referred to as a run or vocal gymnastics.

Run

When a succession of notes is sung, quite often at speed, this is known as a 'run'. In classical singing, these runs show off the flexibility of the voice, and multiple runs in a song are called *coloratura*.

When riffs (see above) or runs are inserted into a song, it's called ornamentation.

The word 'run' is often used for a more formal, planned ornament. A riff is thought to be more of a spontaneous run. Either word can be used.

Scale

A scale is 'a group of notes taken in ascending or descending order'. In vocal coaching, we often practise these ascending or descending patterns in order to warm up our voices or to exercise the muscles. It is also a way of developing our 'musical ear' by repeated practising of the same intervals.

Soft Palate

The posterior fleshy portion of the roof of the mouth. It forms a movable muscular flap that seals off the nasopharynx during swallowing and speech. Also known as the velum or muscular palate

Squillo

A technical term for the resonant trumpet-like sound in the voices of opera singers, this technique can be used by any singer who wants 'ring', 'ping' and 'brilliance' while avoiding a harsh, shrill sound.

Support

This is the term used to describe the appropriate type of breathing which can be used to totally control your voice, enabling it to have the freedom to do whatever is needed.
    Good support comes from great breath control.

Sustain

Sustained singing is singing which carries from one note to another, or notes which can be held in a balanced, unpushed way.

Sustained singing requires good breath control and an ease of vocal production.

Vibrato

'A slight, rapid, and regular fluctuation in the pitch of a note.'

Vocal Folds

Also known as vocal cords, these are folds of mucous membrane stretched horizontally, from back to front, across the larynx. They vibrate, modulating the flow of air being expelled from the lungs during phonation (the production of vocal sounds).

Vocalise

A vocalise is a vocal exercise with no words that is sung on vowels.

Happy Learning, Happy Singing!

If you have got to the end of this book, whether by reading every word or skimming through the chapters, well done and thank you for bearing with me. Singing technique can be dull and may seem a bit like schoolwork, but if you want to make singing your career, it's essential for voice health and will help so much when it comes to getting your voice to do what you want it to. I hope you have already found some of my techniques and advice useful, and once it becomes automatic to look after your voice properly, there will be no looking back. I've tried to explain everything as well as I can without hearing or seeing you, but remember, I'm not a doctor and I can't see inside your throat and see what you're actually doing. Everything I have written is only my opinion. Please remember that while voices can be incredibly resilient, voice damage can take months to repair, and in the worst-case scenario, can be permanent. If you're not sure about anything you've read, and especially if you feel any pain or discomfort when singing or afterwards, please try to see a singing teacher in person. Alternatively, if you think it's a throat problem, you could go and see your GP. Unfortunately, although I can advise you, I can't see or hear any of your bad habits.

I do teach privately and sometimes do workshops or talks, so I will keep you posted about those on my website. Also, there's an email address on there if any of you want to let me know how you're getting on.

YES, YOU CAN SING!

I'm passionate about singing and singers, and I hope I've helped lots of you to start to understand your voices better.

Happy learning, happy singing!

Much love,

Yvie xx

WHAT YVIE MEANS TO ME

'Yvie is the dream voice coach: she's got a handle on every style of singing and brings huge experience and enthusiasm to the party. Whatever level you're at, whether beginner or seasoned pro, Yvie's all-round approach will help you find tone and range you didn't know you had.'

Alexander Armstrong, singer, TV presenter and actor

'I met Yvie while working in the West End on Andrew Lloyd Webber's musical, *Love Never Dies*. I immediately loved her energy, how safe and taken care of she made me feel and how vocally intelligent she is. I think Yvie's extraordinary at what she does and is the kindest human on top of all of it! I remember when I had been out of the show sick and was trying to come back in. I was feeling scared and vulnerable and unsure if I could do it. But she came in especially for me that night, to help me warm up and give me the assurance I needed to get on that stage. I adore Yvie, and anyone who gets to work with her is the luckiest!'

Sierra Boggess, West End and
Broadway leading lady

'The most important thing I learnt from Yvie was discipline, and I had a great rapport with the lovely lady.'

Susan Boyle, *Britain's Got Talent*
runner-up in 2009

'Yvie is an inspiration for young singers today.'

Sarah Brightman

'I had two strong women behind me cheering me on. One was my mum; the other was Yvie, who always had a lot of faith in me. To this day, I still use the ten-minute warm-up she created for me to run through before each show.'

Alexandra Burke, *The X Factor*
winner in 2008

WHAT YVIE MEANS TO ME

'Yvie Burnett is without doubt one of the world's best singing teachers. Her unique approach to teaching, coupled with her ability to cut to the chase and give laser-sharp direction and feedback, makes her one of the most in-demand coaches in the UK and beyond. She also happens to be one of the loveliest people you could ever hope to meet, as I know from having worked with her in my capacity as the voice of *X Factor*, the unseen person who makes all the announcements.'

Peter Dickson, voiceover artist

'I had the pleasure of working with Yvie when I entered *The X Factor* in 2005. She was very supportive of me throughout my journey and taught me how to sustain my voice, taking me to the semi-finals of the competition. I've always found Yvie to be very easy to talk to and understand, and to this day I still call on her when I need further vocal help.'

Brenda Edwards, *The X Factor* contestant in 2005

'Yvie was my true mentor on *X Factor*. She's a fantastic vocal coach. She not only guides you through the notes, she helps you to open up your voice to its maximum potential. And she supports you through your nerves. She's the best!'

Rebecca Ferguson, singer and *The X Factor* contestant

'I first met Yvie on *Superstar*, where she was the vocal coach. She was amazing. I'm absolutely convinced I couldn't have survived that process without her. She filled me with confidence and she really taught me how to structure a song. You shouldn't give everything in the first verse, she said, because that will leave you with nowhere else to go. A song is a story and it has an arc. You also have to establish what is known as the "money note": that point in the song when you open your lungs and the audience starts clapping. Even if it's a small, sad song like Tracy Chapman's "Fast Car", Yvie showed me the moment where I could shine. You have to give the panel, the audience, the people watching at home a little light and shade.'

Ben Forster, *Superstar* winner in 2012

'Yvie has a real gift for finding the potential in a voice. She's worked with the biggest stars in the world and if you want to hit the big notes, read this book!'

Nigel Hall, executive producer of *The X Factor* and *Britain's Got Talent*

'Yvie has the wonderful ability to help you find better vocal placement when singing. That allows you to free your voice and hit the notes you want to sing with ease and support.'

Matt Henry, West End star and *The Voice UK* contestant

'In my short time working with Yvie, I learnt how important breathing is. Of course I'd heard that many times before, but it wasn't until my time with her that I was really made conscious of it. The favourite exercise she showed me was the one lying on my back. I try to do that daily to ensure I am supporting my voice and giving it as much stability as possible.'

TJ Jackson, member of boy band 3T and
nephew of the late great Michael Jackson

'Yvie has a fantastic attention to detail and won't accept anything less than perfect. There's nothing she doesn't understand about music, but what she's also able to do is put your personality into a chosen song – and then coax the best from you. Judges are forever encouraging contestants to make a song their own. Yvie has the rare ability to help you achieve precisely that. In a nutshell, she can make you the best version of you.'

Myleene Klass, singer (Hear'Say), pianist,
model and TV and radio presenter

'One of the best things I took away from working with Yvie was to always support and ground myself, especially on the top notes. It also gives me a firm tummy, which is a nice bonus!'

Leona Lewis, *The X Factor* winner in 2006

'Yvie is the world's leading vocal coach.'

Andrew Lloyd Webber

'Yvie had a big say in terms of song choices on X *Factor*. The great thing about working with her was her calming influence. She was a constant in the madness going on all around, which was exactly what I needed because I was living away from home in this big bubble, the most intense experience of my life.'

Joe McElderry, *The X Factor*
winner in 2009

'I have seen Yvie give singers the confidence to achieve incredible performances.'

Dannii Minogue, singer, dancer, songwriter,
model, actress and TV judge

'Yvie is just incredible. When we first met in 2009 during X *Factor*, and from the first day to the last, she was not just mine but every singer on the show's rock. She always made you feel super-confident, especially before you were about to sing; her attention to detail with everyone was brilliant. Lots of us singers have our own insecurities with our voices, and Yvie makes you forget those issues. She refocuses you on the positives and what you need to do to improve. Love her to bits and always will.'

Olly Murs, pop star and TV presenter

'Yvie very quickly became my rock whilst working on *The Voice* UK. She gave me endless confidence in my ability which allowed me to grow. She taught me a lot about integrity and the importance of standing my ground when necessary.

'Yvie is a mentor and a friend, I wouldn't be where I am without her guidance - pure and simple. She's also an awesome duet partner for everything from *Lakmé* to Bizet to 'The Lonely Goatherd'!

Lucy O'Byrne – Runner-up on The Voice UK
and West End performer

'I first started working with Yvie soon after being selected for the live rounds of *Britain's Got Talent*. Coaching with her was the first tuition I'd had for nearly five years. I found Yvie fun and easy to work with – and everything explained in that soft Aberdonian accent! She trained as an opera singer, which meant that she knew a lot about what I was doing, particularly the technical differences between opera singing, pop and theatre singing. Opera singers don't really use 'belt' singing in the way that pop and theatre singers do; we use head and chest voice and the intermediate area. The so-called *passaggio* is one of the most difficult things to manage technically. Yvie helped me particularly with this by encouraging me to imagine swallowing a hot potato to help lower the larynx.'

Paul Potts, *Britain's Got Talent* winner in 2007

'Yvie is the most wonderful singing teacher. She has given me so much confidence and helps me protect and work as hard as possible on keeping my instrument strong and healthy.

Beautiful energy, beautiful person.'

Sam Smith

'I had the pleasure of working alongside Yvie for many years at *The X Factor* UK. Apart from her energy and fun loving spirit she coached from dawn 'til dusk in killer Louboutin heels, making the studio a happier place while genuinely increasing the vocal ranges and techniques of the singers without losing their unique styles. Any singer that works with her will improve in both areas and also grow in confidence knowing they really CAN hit those notes once she teaches them how to do it!'

Sinitta – Popstar and mentor on *The X Factor*

WHAT YVIE MEANS TO ME

'I enjoy working with Yvie. She really knows how to get those high notes out of me!'

Nicole Scherzinger, pop star and
The X Factor judge

'Yvie is my voice angel. If I ever need to rehearse for something important or want to brush up on my singing, I go straight to her. She gave me the confidence and self-belief I have today, and stopped me from wishing I'd be swallowed into a black hole every time I stepped on stage. Not only is she my singing guru but also such a dear and important friend who has supported me through every stage of my singing career, from the O2 to panto. Everybody needs an Yvie!'

Stacey Solomon, *The X Factor* contestant in
2009 and presenter on ITV's *Loose Women*

'Yvonne and I shared the same enthusiasm and hard work and dedication while studying at the Guildhall School of Music & Drama. Learning a vast repertoire in many languages and different styles, from early music to opera, from jazz to the simplest of folk songs, enhanced our perception of how the human voice behaves. Trial and error within style and interpretation was the best way to work on the voice technically, and then everything seemed to fall into place with breathing, musicality, posture, diction. Yvie was certainly a hard worker, and that was evident in the development of her beautiful voice from the first day she walked into the Guildhall.'

Sir Bryn Terfel, one of the world's
greatest opera singers

'I honestly don't think I'd have won *X Factor* without Yvie.'
Shayne Ward, *The X Factor* winner in 2005

'I met Yvie a decade into my career, by which time I'd picked up bad habits – all of which she shook out of me. Working on these things has made life so much easier. If you're a singer, you're not on your own; there should always be a team to help, as there is in the rest of my life. Mechanics fix my car. Larry cuts my hair. Yvie keeps me singing.'

Ricky Wilson, frontman of Kaiser Chiefs
and former judge on *The Voice UK*

WHAT YVIE MEANS TO ME

Above: 'Having fun working with the gorgeous Sam Smith.' © *James Barber*

Left: 'Hanging out with Gary Barlow backstage.'

YES, YOU CAN SING!

'Myself with Leona Lewis and Alexandra Burke (*X Factor* winners in 2006 and 2008) in Los Angeles at the Sunset Tower Hotel.'

'In the studio with Nicole Scherzinger.'

WHAT YVIE MEANS TO ME

'Despite being a Hollywood star, Glenn Close is one of the most
down-to-earth people I've worked with!'

'Myself with *X Factor* winner Joe McElderry and Ben Forster, winner of *Superstar*.'

'With the lovely Susan Boyle.'

'On the *X Factor* set with Louis Walsh – the man who changed my career.'

ACKNOWLEDGEMENTS

First, I would like to thank my writing partner, Richard Barber, without whom there would be no book. I will miss our endless meetings at my kitchen table, helped by a supply of bagels. After a few red wines, your Danny Dyer impersonation is legendary!

Nick Fiveash, thank you for introducing Richard and me, and for your continued support.

Thank you to John Blake and James Hodgkinson at John Blake Publishing, who saw the potential of the project from the moment we met and for all your effort in getting this book onto the shelves, as well as Jane Donovan and Amy Mather for your editing expertise. An extra thank you to Sarah Fortune for your hard work and endless patience. Thanks also to the lovely balls of energy, enthusiasm and expertise who are Ellis Keene and Lizzie Dorney-

Kingdom at Bonnier Publishing and to Mark Hollinshead at Hollicom for always believing in me.

Special thanks to Graeme Lauren, who read all my technical chapters to make sure I made sense! Thank you for your input and thank you for being one of my oldest and dearest friends. Also to another incredibly supportive friend, the musical genius that is producer Nigel Wright. A very big thank you to John Rubin who has reassured so many of my singers over the years with his expert advice.

To every single one of the contributors to this book, including all my incredible singers of whom I'm so fond, I'm so proud to have all your quotes included... Thank you.

Thank you to my incredibly supportive family, Gordon, Emily and Ollie. I can't talk about you or I will cry: you are my world. And not forgetting the cuddles from the cats, Timple, Rimple and the late Molly, while I sat writing.

Thank you to my wonderful Mum and Dad, who instilled all the practising and perfecting the voice that I have talked about in these chapters. I miss you.

Finally, a special thanks to Louis Walsh, who changed the course of my career. You are a dear and special friend. Love you always.

I'm off for a large glass of something now.

Big kiss to you all,
Yvie xx

CONTACTS LIST AND USEFUL LINKS

The British Voice Association (BVA):
http://www.britishvoiceassociation.org.uk/
The British Wheel of Yoga: https://www.bwy.org.uk/
The Chartered Society of Physiotherapy (CSP):
http://www.csp.org.uk/

The Health and Care Professions Council (HCPC):
http://www.hcpc-uk.co.uk/
Music for Youth: http://www.mfy.org.uk/
The National Center for Voice and Speech at the
University of Utah's YouTube channel (developers of
the 'straws exercise discussed in Chapter 7):
 https://www.youtube.com/user/NCVS456
Sing Up: www.singup.org
Yvie's website: www.yvieburnett.com